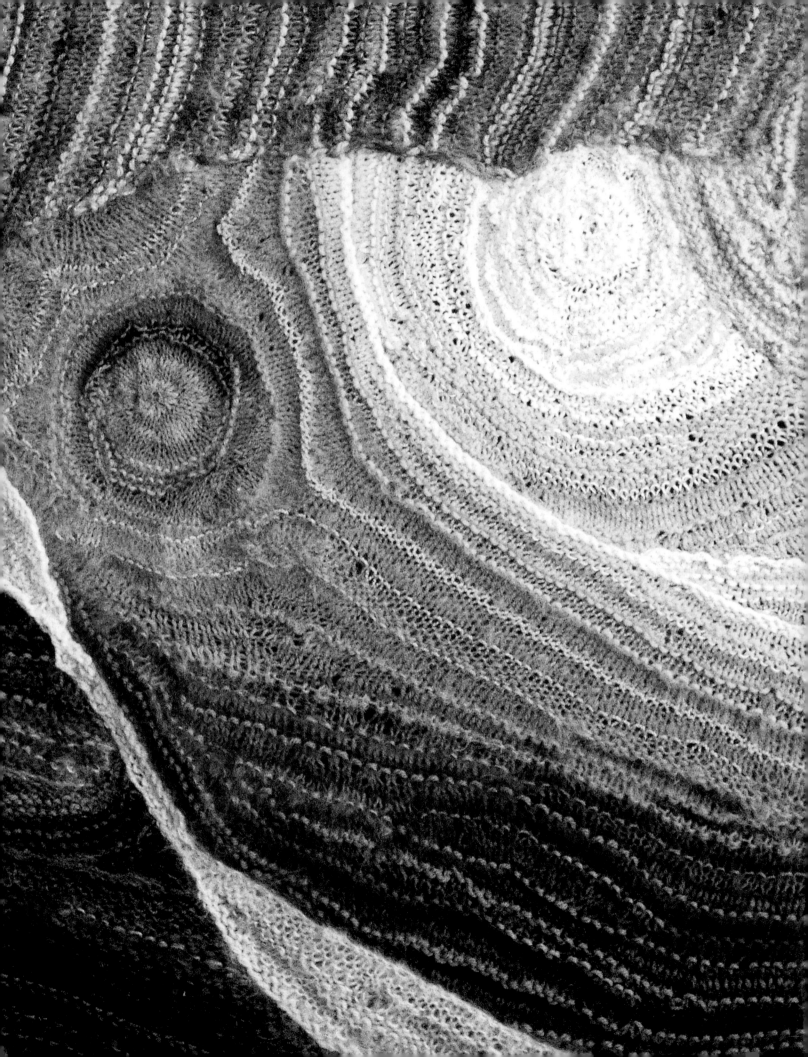

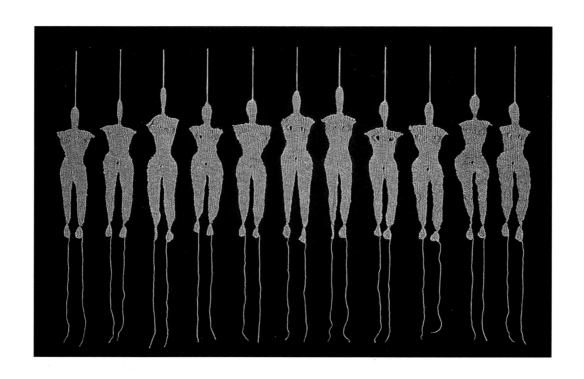

Knitting Art

150 Innovative Works from
18 Contemporary Artists

Karen Searle

Voyageur Press

Frontis:

Doppo Italia | Carolyn Halliday | 2002 | hand-knit copper and aluminum wires, brass wire filling | 14" tall
Carolyn's double-layer wire torso celebrates the beauty of imperfect female bodies. *Photograph by Petronella Ytsma*

Title, main:

Living Cave | Debbie New | 1995 | handknit in mixed fibers | 3' x 4'
Debbie's visit to slot canyons in Arizona inspired this interpretation in stitches.

Title, inset:

No Strings Attached | Adrienne Sloane | 2006 | machine-knit linen rug warp | 37" h x 47"
Adrienne created this knitted installation as an ironic feminist statement.

Contents:

Sense Spin | Janet Morton | 2000 | hand-knit audio cassette tape
Janet created this piece for *Persistent Melody*, a gallery installation on the theme of music and memory. The cassette-tape tornado, embellished with feather monarchs, is suspended over a record turntable.

First published in 2008 by Voyageur Press, an imprint of MBI Publishing Company, 400 1st Avenue North, Suite 300, Minneapolis, MN 55401 USA

Copyright © 2008 by Karen Searle

Voyageur Press titles are also available at discounts in bulk quantity for industrial or sales-promotional use. For details write to Special Sales Manager at MBI Publishing Company, 400 1st Avenue North, Suite 300, Minneapolis, MN 55401 USA.

To find out more about our books, join us online at www.voyageurpress.com.

ISBN-13: 978-0-7603-3067-8

Editor: Kari Cornell
Designer: Sara Holle

Printed in China

Library of Congress Cataloging-in-Publication Data

Searle, Karen.
  Knitting art : 150 innovative works from 18 contemporary artists / Karen Searle.
    p. cm.
  Includes index.
  ISBN 978-0-7603-3067-8 (hb, w/ jkt)
  1. Knitting. I. Title.
  TT820.S44 2008
  746.43'041—dc22

                    2007050424

Acknowledgments

A great many thanks go to the seventeen artists included in this book who graciously allowed me to spend time with them. I am grateful to Kari Cornell and Michael Dregni of Voyageur Press, who bravely and enthusiastically took on this topic and have made the entire authoring process a delight. Thanks also to Melanie Falick for having the insight to requisition an article on this subject back in 2001. I greatly appreciate the help and encouragement I have received for this project from Doroth Mayer, Lindsay Obermeyer, Suzanne Baizerman, Sarah Quinton, Ruth Scheuing, Carrie Lederer, Liz Collins, Arline Fisch, Janet Lipkin, Rob Hillestad, W. David Phillips, and Patricia Abrahamian. I am also grateful to my students and to the many artist-knitters who have been keeping me informed about their work over the years.

Homage to the Goddess, Creation | Karen Searle | tablet-woven silk, metallic threads, and beads knitted and crocheted around a chair frame One of a series of goddess thrones, this chair honors creation myths and legends from many cultures in a folk-art style. *Photograph by Karen Searle*

Contents

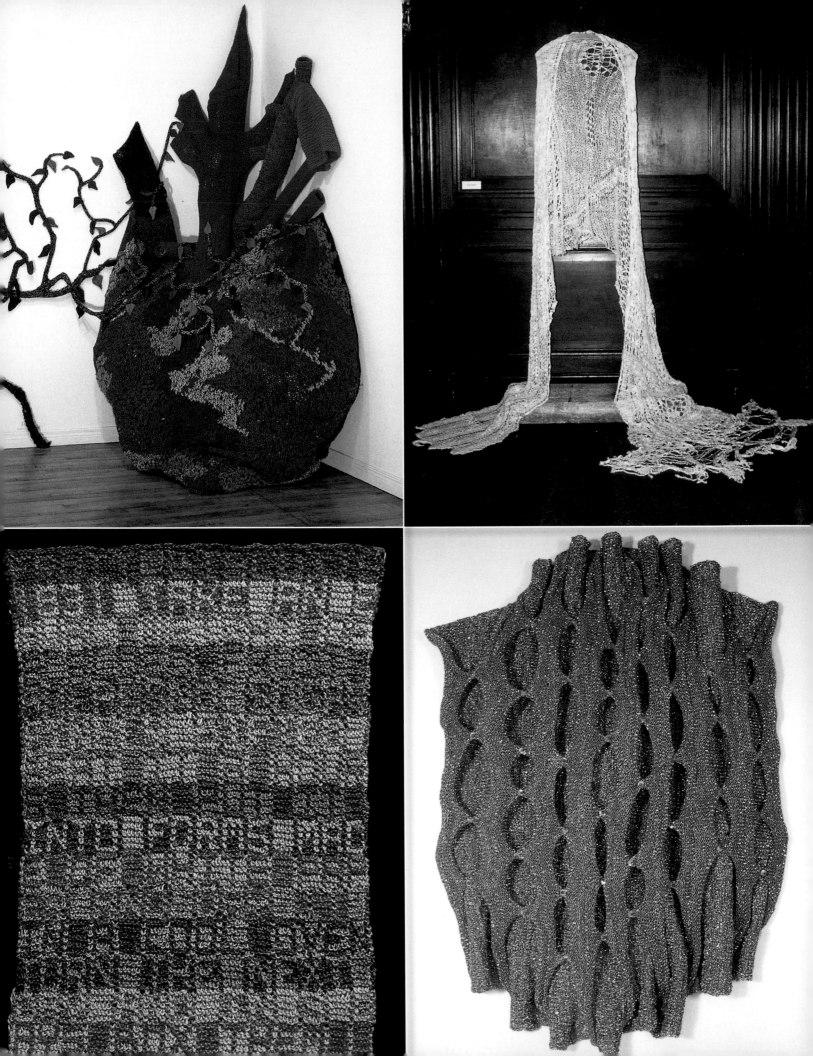

Introduction

Symbolism can be read into each stitch—it is a loop without beginning or end. Interconnected loops can be a metaphor for life and human connectedness.
—Karen Searle

Although the technique of knitting with knitting needles has existed for about 900 years as a practical means of making clothing and household textiles, only rarely was it used conceptually before the 1960s, when a small number of artists began to explore knitting for its artistic potential. That number grew slowly during the 1970s and 1980s in the United States; somewhat more rapidly in Europe and the UK. Now, with a resurgence of interest in knitting during the past decade, new and longtime knitters have been revitalizing the craft and expanding its creative possibilities. As an artist who has created knitted art objects for some thirty years, I have been fascinated by how conceptual fiber artists have approached knitting and especially how some artists have used knitting techniques to explore the meaning of "women's work" or domestic textile practices.

What is sparking the renewed interest in knitting, and why are more and more knitters venturing into utilizing knitting as a conceptual art form? There are multiple reasons. New publications, an abundance of yarn shops, and the rise of knitting circles and community knitting projects all have supported the renaissance. The evolution of technology, including Internet sites and weblogs, has connected knitters in new ways and stimulated a flow of ideas. Renewed interest in the domestic arts and in the handmade among artists and art students has widened the parameters of what is possible, as they adapt and reinvent knitting to suit their expressive purposes. And performance-based artists place knitting in the public arena with projects that involve audience interaction.

With the increasing popularity of knitting as a medium for artistic expression also comes a welcomed increase in the number of art galleries willing to exhibit knitting, crochet, and embroidery as art. The most significant validation for art knitting so far in the United States resulted from an international exhibition, Radical Lace and Subversive Knitting, held at the Museum of American Design in New York in 2007. Carrie Lederer, curator of the

Top, left: **Tending** | Janet Morton | 2003 | hand-knit heart, vines, and leaves, 2500 recycled soda bottles | 12' tall

Top, right: **Portrait of Alzheimers** | Katharine Cobey | 1992 | knit of handspun silk and wool, stabile, wood base, hanger | 69" h x 77" w x 28" d

Bottom, left: **Fruit** from the handknitted "letters" series | John Krynick | knitted thread | 6" x 8"

Bottom, right: **Channels** from the "Channels and Openings" series | Donna Lish | 2005 | two machine-knitted layers stitched together | 23" h x 16" w x 1.5" d

Collar | Arline Fisch | 1985 | machine-knit coated copper wire and fine silver wire with a handmade sterling clasp | 6.5" w x 14" l x 9.5" diameter
Arline drew inspiration for this elaborate neckpiece from Elizabethan fashion.

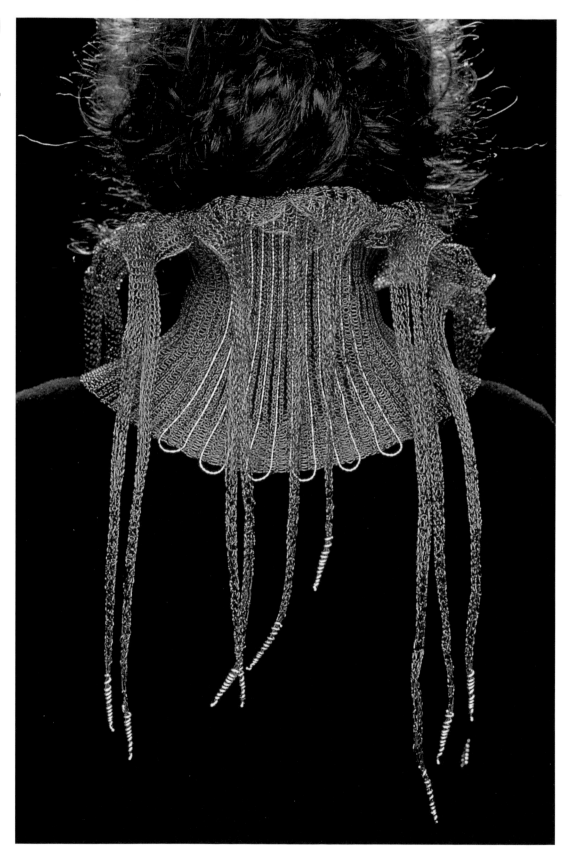

art movement in the United States. She studied painting at the Pratt Institute in New York in the late 1960s but became more interested in exploring color and form through crochet, creating dramatic, textural garments that transformed the wearer into a living sculpture. Janet completed her BFA degree work with her fiber explorations, feeling as if she had discovered her art. She continued to produce improvisational crocheted costumes after relocating to the San Francisco Bay area. In 1976, she received a Fulbright scholarship to study textile-making techniques in Ghana. That experience focused her attention on flat textiles and garments with graphic content. On returning home, she began using a knitting machine to explore her design ideas.

With the machine and a brilliant palette of her own hand-dyed yarns, color and graphics became the focal points of her knitted garments; her designs were influenced by the natural world and by primitive cultures. Her knitwear was also sculptural, involving complex shapes and constructions. She often produced a series of five to ten garments based on the same graphic imagery or color theme. Janet's work has been exhibited and published widely and has appeared in numerous books, most recently in *Artwear: Fashion and Anti-Fashion* by Melissa Leventon and *Craft in America* by Jo Lauria and Steve Fenton. After a ten-year hiatus from textile-making during the 1990s, when she turned her attention to painting and printmaking, Janet has returned to creating fiber art with spectacular one-of-a-kind hand-knit and felted coats and jackets.

Artist and educator Robert Hillestad was creating spectacular hand-knit kimonos, capes, and shawls during the height of the wearable art movement. His dramatic, richly textured, knitted-pile works were jazz compositions in color and motion, inspired by the rhythm and movement of dance and emphasizing the aesthetic characteristics of his unusual fiber combinations. He worked novelty yarns, fabric strips, ribbon, tape, and thread into compelling surfaces using a looped stitch structure. He finds knitting "a collaborative activity, one hand helping the other, one set of fingers and a thumb responding to the other. I enjoy the sensation of having yarn, ribbon, tape, thread, and combinations thereof pass through my hands en route to being manipulated into stitches."

Robert's fiber works in various media have been exhibited widely in the United States and abroad. He earned degrees in art and design at the University of Wisconsin-Madison and Drexel University in Philadelphia, and a doctorate in textiles and clothing at The Ohio State University. He did post-graduate work at the Art Institute of Chicago and is a graduate of École de la Chambre Syndicale de la Couture in Paris. When he retired in 1996 from a thirty-one-year career in design education in the Department of Textiles, Clothing, and Design at the University of Nebraska–Lincoln, the university's Robert Hillestad Textiles Gallery was named in his honor. In 2008, the Friends of the Robert Hillestad Textiles Gallery mounted a retrospective exhibition and published a monograph on his artwork. Robert's teaching and exhibitions have influenced many handknitters to be adventurous in creating unique designs.

Recent Innovations

Knitting's history as a portable and community-based craft invites artists to bring it into public and community settings through performance and other interactive means. One example of this is *Knitting Nation*, an ongoing, collaborative performance and site-specific installation organized by fashion knitwear designer Liz Collins in an effort to publicly explore aspects of nationalism, globalism, and community. Her "armies" of uniformed machine knitters and sewers knit and assemble giant banners on-site at public festivals. In another example, designer Cat Mazza challenges corporations that use sweatshop labor through the issue-based Internet project microrevolt.org. The site offers visitors a chance to participate in group petitions by knitting or crocheting a square for a huge mural. And, in a "guerrilla-knitting" practice—called "tagging" in the United States and "viral knitting" in Canada—knitters secretly adorn their environments by placing colorful knitted coverings on car antennas, lampposts, gates, and trees. The limited-edition magazine, *Knitknit,* published by Sabrina Gschwandtner keeps tabs on avant garde artists working in knit and crochet. As an example of increased general public acceptance of all aspects of knitting, during winter 2007, the city of Chicago held a three-month "Stitching Salon" event featuring knitting and stitchery-related demonstrations, classes and family activities, and interactive knitting performances by such artists as Anni Holm and her "Musical Knitting Band." This is, indeed, an exciting time for knitters.

The Artists

Knitting's versatility appeals to artists who may use the craft to honor the history and tradition of women's work or to raise questions about femininity,

Santa Fe in my Dreams
coat | Janet Lipkin | 1987
| machine-knit, hand-dyed wool and silk
The imagery for this coat came to Janet in a dream. It combines African-inspired motifs with adobe forms and soft colors. Janet recalls that the shaping came from a desire "to do something based on a feeling of purity—I discovered the square." The coat is in the collection of the Museum of Art and Design, New York.
Photograph by Barry Shapiro

Bloom | Janet Lipkin | 2004 | hand-knit felted wool
Bloom is knitted in a technique that Janet calls "puzzle knitting." First, she drew the design and made a full-scale graph on knitting paper. She knit the garment in sections, tracing each section according to the design of the garment and the direction of her knitting. The coat was sold by Julie Artisans Gallery in New York. Janet says, "The content is something I am still working on: the joy and fragility of life, the flower symbolizing new growth and change." *Photograph by Barry Shapiro*

Celebration Cape | Robert Hillestad, hand-knit mixed yarns and fabric strips with knitted embellishments
Robert's elegant, textured knits were inspired by dance and movement.

Celebration Coat #1 | Robert Hillestad | hand-knit mixed fibers and fabric strips
Robert worked his highly textured materials in a looped stitch to create a reversible fabric with pile on the outside and a striped design on the inside.

masculinity, and domesticity. A conceptual work can evoke knitting's associations with adornment and the body, memories of comfort and warmth, and expressions of love and caring. The repetitive and meditative process of knitting can be used ritually in performance as a form of healing. In a detailed, or large-scale work, knitting can raise questions about time and productivity and how these are valued in Western society.

In *Knitting Art*, I am pleased to introduce a group of North American artists who choose to communicate their artistic observations about our lives, humanity, and interconnectedness through knitting. Although regretfully I cannot include everyone who is doing exciting work in knitting here, I can provide a snapshot of the current art knitting scene. This book includes several fiber artists who have explored knitting's artistic potential since the 1980s: Kathryn Alexander, Katharine Cobey, Barb Hunt, Donna Lish, and myself; others who were trained in various fine art disciplines and are putting knitting to unexpected new uses: Lisa Anne Auerbach, Reina Mia Brill, Ilisha Helfman, Laura Kamian, John Krynick, Anna Maltz, Janet Morton, Mark Newport, Lindsay Obermeyer, and Jeung-Hwa Park; and still others who have gravitated to knitting art after enjoying careers in other fields: Carolyn Halliday, Debbie New, and Adrienne Sloane. All of these artists share one characteristic: they approach knitting with a sense of curiosity and wonder. Enjoy this rare glimpse into their art, their minds, and their knitting lives.

Knitting Nation | a performance project organized by Liz Collins, MOMA | 2005

Knitting Nation explores aspects of textile and apparel manufacturing, laying bare the process of making knitted fabric. At each of its venues, Knitting Nation's team of workers produces a banner appropriate to the event on manually operated knitting machines. In its 2005 appearance at New York's Museum of Modern Art, the team of uniformed machine knitters and stitchers knit and assembled a giant American flag that covered the side of the museum building.

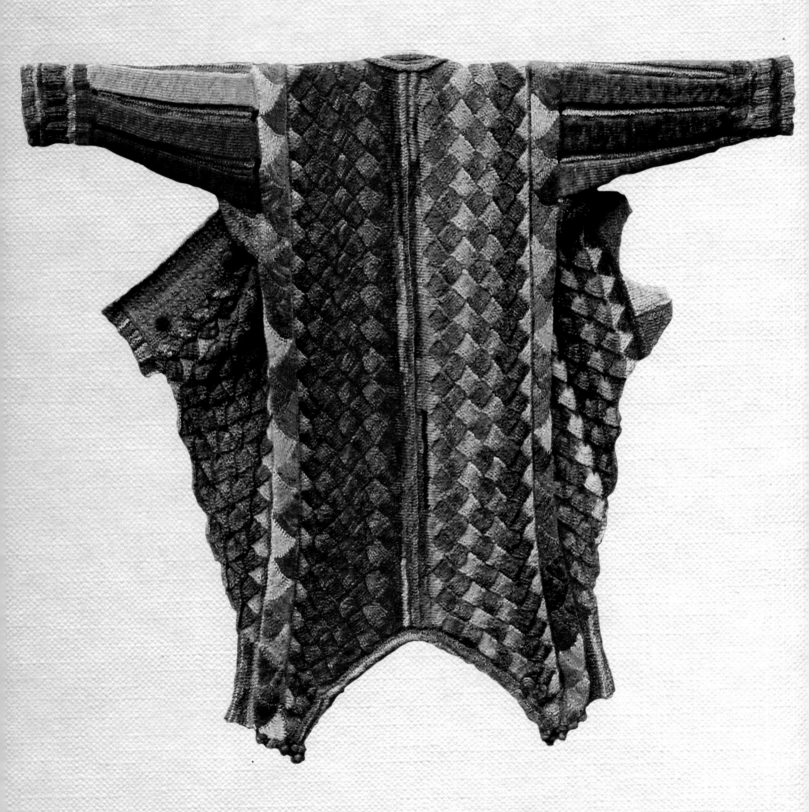

Kathryn Alexander

Kathryn Alexander,
wearing one of her
sculptural entrelac hats.

Kathryn Alexander uses handspun yarn to create amazing mosaic garments and hats in jewel-like hues. Her work is characterized by vibrant, asymmetrical arrangements of tiny interlocking squares and triangles set against tranquil areas of striping. Her works can be worn but are equally spectacular mounted on the wall and in gallery exhibitions.

Kathryn's two main forms of expression are handknitting and weaving. Her handspinning and dyeing impart a distinctive identity to her work. Much of art is an attempt to provide visual answers to probing questions, and Kathryn experienced an epiphany when, tired of working with commercially made yarns, she asked herself, "What happens if I change the material?" The answer propelled her into a lifelong exploration of the effects of handspun, "energized" yarns in her garments and fabrics. Not only are her unique yarns energized, her colors and designs are lively and energetic, as well. In Kathryn's hands ordinary stitches to take on mysterious qualities as rectangles become swirls and the swirls stand up in three-dimensional peaks.

Kathryn takes great pride in being a spinner, since it is the yarn that makes the cloth. "When you twist fibers that are straight to hold them together, the spinning creates energy, causing the yarn to twist back on itself," she explains. "I need to make my own yarns because I can make any size, any fiber, any color."

The designs in Kathryn's knits grow organically through her intuitive, multidirectional knitting style. She casts on with whatever color she happens to pick up and works in small units. When she completes one color section, she chooses a harmonious color, picks up stitches along an edge, and knits out in a new direction. Some of her garments combine areas of machine knitting and handknitting.

But it's the dyeing of the yarns that holds the most excitement for her. At first she tried using natural dyes, believing that chemical dyeing required knowledge of

Coat | Kathryn Alexander | 2005 | hand-knit, handspun, hand-dyed energized yarn
Kathryn builds her garments section by section, knitting each new segment onto the preceding one. For this coat, areas of entrelac squares are arranged next to areas of triangles and strips of plain knitting.

chemistry. Later she learned a simple chemical dyeing method that enables her to dye as many as eighty shades of wool in one session. Occasionally she dyes her machine-knit yardage using shibori, or resist-patterning, techniques.

Kathryn grew up on a Wisconsin farm where she acquired a love of horses; they have been her companions throughout her life. She was surrounded by textile-making activities. Her mother and aunts are lifelong knitters, and her mother also spins and weaves. In her early twenties, Kathryn worked planting trees for a paper company in Washington State and learned to knit from another female worker. After a move to Berkeley, California, she learned to weave and became active in the Bay area fiber community. When her husband's job took them to Pittsburgh, Pennsylvania, she discovered another strong fiber arts community there. She now resides in upstate New York.

Kathryn researched *collapse-weave fabrics* (fabrics woven from yarns spun in opposite directions) while in Berkeley and was fascinated by the effect that yarn twist has on woven fabric. In an early weaving experiment, she noticed a knit-like effect that resulted from placing an *S-twist* yarn and a *Z-twist* yarn side-by-side. She then started to explore the effect of manipulating yarn twist in hand-knit fabrics, with amazing results. The energized singles yarn affects the stitch structure, sometimes dramatically. "Experienced knitters couldn't tell what it was," she said. "It is remarkable what energy yarn does to a knit surface. The garter stitch looked like little triangles, and it also looked like double-layer."

After trying out her energized yarns in traditional knit surfaces, Kathryn tried them with entrelac, a textural knitted surface. The *entrelac* knitting technique, which consists of rows of squares knit on opposing bias, provides an excellent vehicle for her textural symphonies. "No new skills are needed, I just have to think in a new way," she explains. Using plied or balanced yarn for entrelac yields a flat surface, while Kathryn's surfaces are deeply dimensional and "alive" with peaks and swirls. She also discovered that the direction of knitting can work with, or in opposition to, the direction of the yarn's twist to cause different surface effects. "Something always happens to shift me in another direction. That keeps it exciting for me—there are always new ideas."

While mastering the entrelac technique, Kathryn recalls, "I came to the conclusion that you really should listen to your mother. I was making my first pair of entrelac socks, and my mom said, 'I really think you should weave those ends in as you go.' And I just wanted to keep knitting. When I finished, I had fifty to sixty ends to weave in, and it took me a whole afternoon. So now I listen to my mother and weave them in as I go."

Kathryn and her husband, Mark, live in a 160-year-old farmhouse on fifteen acres of land north of Troy, New York. Her garments and sculptural hats adorn each room. In an upstairs gallery, she displays the ski sweaters that her mother had knit for her and her siblings when they were children and young adults, "keeping alive the memories of our experiences wearing them."

Kathryn recently incorporated her studio into the house when the old studio building on the property had to be torn down. The farmhouse is a hive of activity as this weaver, spinner, dyer, artist, writer, teacher, and businesswoman designs, creates, and exhibits her art works and assembles kits for her sweater designs. There are also three horses and a large garden to take care of.

With so many demands on her time, Kathryn has to work efficiently. She does all of the spinning, dyeing, knitting, and weaving for her art clothing. She needs about 16,000 yards of handspun yarn for the warp and weft in a woven piece. Spinning such quantities requires speed, precision, and good tools. She uses efficient dyeing practices but then is quite willing to spend incalculable amounts of time knitting or weaving very detailed works.

A few years ago, Kathryn started producing kits for some of her garment designs (available on her website, www.kathrynalexander.net). Each year she visits her brother's sheep ranch in Montana to sort and select fleeces to be spun during the coming year's kit production. The Green Mountain Spinnery in Vermont spins the fleece into a singles yarn according to her specifications, and this yarn behaves much like Kathryn's own handspun. She dyes it at home in her trademark range of brilliant hues. Then the dining room becomes the kit-assembly room; her mother comes to help skein the wool and assemble the kits.

A popular teacher, Kathryn occasionally travels to present workshops and lectures. She is working on a book about entrelac knitting that offers a freeform approach to designing that uses the reader's own shapes and knit stitches.

Cardigan | Kathryn Alexander
Kathryn dyed her white, handspun, machine-knit yardage using *shibori* resist-patterning techniques. She created seam accents by knitting the pieces together with a three-needle bind-off technique, and embellished the garment with hand stitching.

Kathryn knits for the sheer joy of it. "When you're confident about your working process, whatever you make will be artful," she says. "While I knit, I think about how happy I feel, and feeling good about myself makes all of life seem better. It's not just the knitting that is joyful, it's the colors I use and how I build things section by section, revising as I go—the skirt I'm working on started out as a sweater—that keeps it fun and engaging. There are still new things to discover in knitting. We all bring something different to it. That's what makes our work unique."

Dress | Kathryn Alexander | 2004 | hand-knit, energized handspun single-ply yarn
Kathryn set out to knit a lightweight "swingy" dress using her energized handspun yarn. Then she decided that she needed to use at least fifty colors, because "I wanted to feel happy while I was working on this." She trimmed it with "doodads," her term for the knitted embellishments.

Detail of one of Kathryn's entrelac sweaters knit with her energized handspun yarns

The energized yarn adds dimensionality to the entrelac areas of this sweater knit in Kathryn's handspun yarn.

Star | Kathryn Alexander | hand-knit, handspun, hand-dyed energized yarn
This complex star design comprises the top of one of Kathryn's sculptural hats made using the entrelac technique.

Skirt with Triangles and Doodads | Kathryn Alexander | hand-knit, handspun, hand-dyed energized yarn
Kathryn began to knit a sweater, incorporating about fifty colors, but as the piece progressed she realized "it just had to be a skirt, so I let it. I wanted a swingy, colorful skirt with lots of doodads in it, so I used small triangles and stripes and I-cord circles for accent."

Jeung-Hwa Park

Jeung-Hwa Park with an array of her sculptural scarves. *Photograph by Karen Philippi*

With a subtle balance of content, context, and technique, Jeung-Hwa Park transforms machine-knitted fabric into dimensional, wearable sculptures and conceptual works of art.

She is inspired by the Eastern yin and yang philosophy, which seeks the proper harmonic balance between two principles in continual movement. The disparate elements joined together in her work are those of loose/tight, flat/dimensional, smooth/puckered, and positive/negative textures. In blending ancient techniques with modern technology—hand crafting and machine knitting—along with an innate sense of color and emotion, she unites Eastern and Western philosophies of art. She says, "I bring opposites together in harmony in one piece. It's like me. Sometimes I'm American, sometimes I'm Korean."

Born in Pusan, Korea, Jeung-Hwa studied apparel design and worked as a sportswear designer in Seoul's fashion industry. Her husband's graduate studies brought the couple and their two sons to Rhode Island in 1991. Experiencing culture shock at first, Jeung-Hwa worked part-time as a fashion correspondent for Korean fashion magazines, reporting on American fashion. She enrolled in the Rhode Island School of Design (RISD) to study apparel design but soon decided to pursue an MFA degree in textile design, where she learned hand and machine knitting and became interested in using knitting for wearable art. "There are innovative knitwear designers in Korea," she says, "but handknitting is not part of a young girl's education there."

Her return to school was an effort to combine apparel with textiles: to integrate fashion with the fabric that is its basis. Some of her early classroom experiments involved the handknitting of her own machine-knitted yarns. After experimenting with the Japanese resist-dyeing techniques known collectively as *shibori*, which

Shell | Jeung-Hwa Park | machine-knit, hand-dyed, felted wool and silk | 10" x 60"
A cascade of shell forms covers this narrow felted scarf. The plastic discs that Jeung-Hwa tied into the knitting before dyeing and felting keep the knit stitches intact while the rest of the piece felts. *Photograph by Karen Philippi*

Scarf in process | Jeung-Hwa Park
Jeung-Hwa has bound hazelnuts into the machine-knit fabric to keep the knit stitches visible in those areas. This piece has been dyed and felted and is ready for untying. *Photograph by Karen Philippi*

include stitching, pleating, and gathering fabric before dyeing, she became curious about their effects on machine-knit fabrics.

She credits her teacher and mentor, Maria Tulokas, with helping her to discover her art medium. In response to an assignment to find a common material and invent your own way of working with it, Jeung-Hwa decided to try felting her machine-knit fabric into three-dimensional shapes. To keep some of the knit stitches visible in the felt, she tied chickpeas at intervals into the loosely knit yardage. In the process, she discovered that the stretched stitches in the tied areas did not felt at all. "My teacher left a note that said, 'Keep going,'" she says. The result—Jeung-Hwa's shibori-inspired dyeing technique combined with her felted machine-knit fabric—brings a new aesthetic to knitting.

After graduation, Jeung-Hwa quickly became frustrated with job hunting. She was "too artistic" for textile industry jobs, and teaching jobs were elusive. Acceptance into her first craft show, Crafts at the Castle 2000 in Boston, revealed a possible new career path. She focused on scarf production, happy to be establishing a business while her husband completed his doctorate. Her work can be seen on www.guild.com.

"The scarf occupies a limited space but is unlimited in its potential for exploration," Jeung-Hwa says. Her process has many steps. Starting with fine, white merino wool, she knits an oversized fabric, ties small objects into it, felts it, dyes it, then releases the objects to reveal the textural pattern. The knitted cloth's flexibility allows it to take on the shape of the tied-in object. The rest of the piece felts. She prefers using natural objects such as fava beans, hazelnuts, and peanut shells for sculpting the fabric. For some pieces, she uses a stitch-resistant technique, which yields a flatter, slightly puckered effect resembling drawing. To felt the scarves, Jeung-Hwa boils the knitted piece with its tied-in objects for ten minutes, then puts them through a washing-machine cycle.

After the felting process is complete, Jeung-Hwa dyes the scarf. This is the most exciting part of the process for her, as the color "gives life" to the scarf. Adopting the attitude of a painter, she immerses the scarf in up to six different dye pots to achieve many subtle color gradations. Her large studio fills with color as she hangs the pieces up to dry.

When the pieces are dry, Jeung-Hwa unties the bundles and removes the objects. The results are always surprising and delightful. The tied-off areas form light, airy dimensional imagery against their backgrounds of muted hues. One side has a positive (raised) effect; the other side has indentations. She likes both sides equally. In addition to the scarves and shawls that she produces for art fairs and boutiques, she has found the technique suitable for garments and wall installations.

Jeung-Hwa translates her love of nature and awareness of its cycles of time, aging, and rebirth through her love of color and dyeing. She is entranced with the constantly changing colors of the New England landscape. "The movement of color represents life to me, which captures moment by moment my personal memory," she says. She adapts color schemes from vegetables, trees, the sky, and the

Falling Leaves (L) and **Rain** (R) | Jeung-Hwa Park | machine-knit wool and silk, tied, stitched, felted, and dyed | L: 12" x 70"/R: 12" x 70"
Jeung-Hwa made the leaf shapes in *Falling Leaves* by gathering and stitching the knit fabric tightly before dyeing and felting it. Chickpeas were tied into *Rain* to create a raised design in the felt. *Photograph by Karen Philippi*

Shell (L) and **Rain Drop** (R) | Jeung-Hwa Park | machine-knit wool and silk, tied, stitched, felted, and dyed | L: 10" x 60"/R: 12" x 70"
Flat discs tied into the knitting form the textural pattern in *Shell*. Jeung-Hwa dipped it into a series of dye baths for the color gradation. *Rain Drop*'s pattern motifs were gathered, stitched, and dyed. *Photograph by Karen Philippi*

air. "These qualities inform the circle of life to me metaphorically," she says.

Jeung-Hwa divides her working time between her studio in an old mill building in Pawtucket and her home in nearby Providence. She completes the dyeing and felting processes in her studio and does the knitting at home. She can fit in time at her machine in between her roles as a wife and the mother of two teenaged sons. "I enjoy the artist's life and being a wife," she says, "but the most exciting is being a mother." In addition to a busy exhibition schedule, Jeung-Hwa teaches Korean in a weekend cultural program and teaches a machine knitting class in

RISD's apparel department. She presents occasional workshops on her felting technique.

Jeung-Hwa is happy to be able to apply her design background to knitting. She finds it both a practical and an artistic medium—a vehicle for design effects as well as for artistic expressions. Exhibitions allow her to develop new ideas and to create larger works. She has achieved a kind of balance between creative development and income-generating production work. Her scarves are produced as multiples, yet no two are exactly alike. She expands her concepts little by little, creating a new type of work each spring. "Further development is my challenge," she says.

Waves | Jeung-Hwa Park |
machine-knit wool and silk,
tied, felted, and dyed |
8" x 70"
Chickpeas tied into the knitting
before the dyeing and felting
stages create the raised surface
pattern of waves. *Photograph by
Karen Philippi*

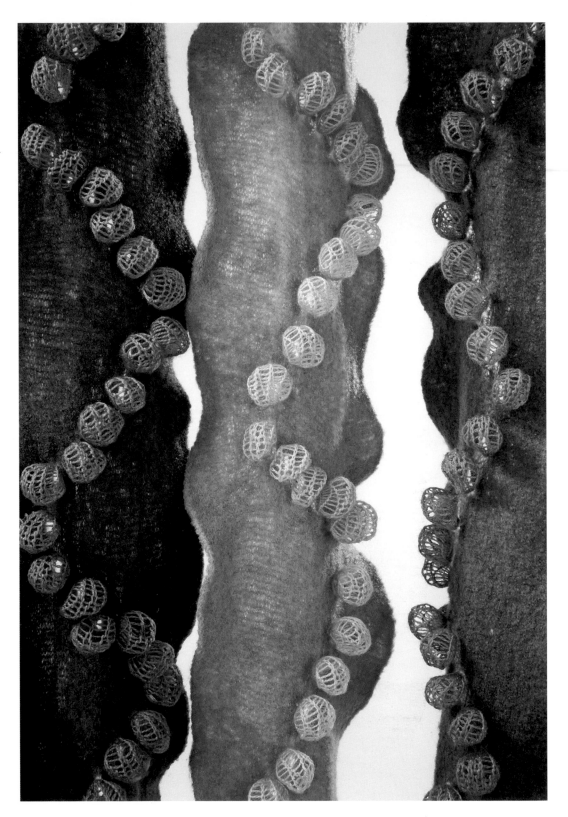

Harvest | Jeung-Hwa Park | machine-knit wool and silk, tied, felted, dyed | 10" x 75" Jeung-Hwa has created two contrasting surfaces in one scarf with her resist-dyeing technique. This fabric was felted only slightly after dyeing. *Photograph by Karen Philippi*

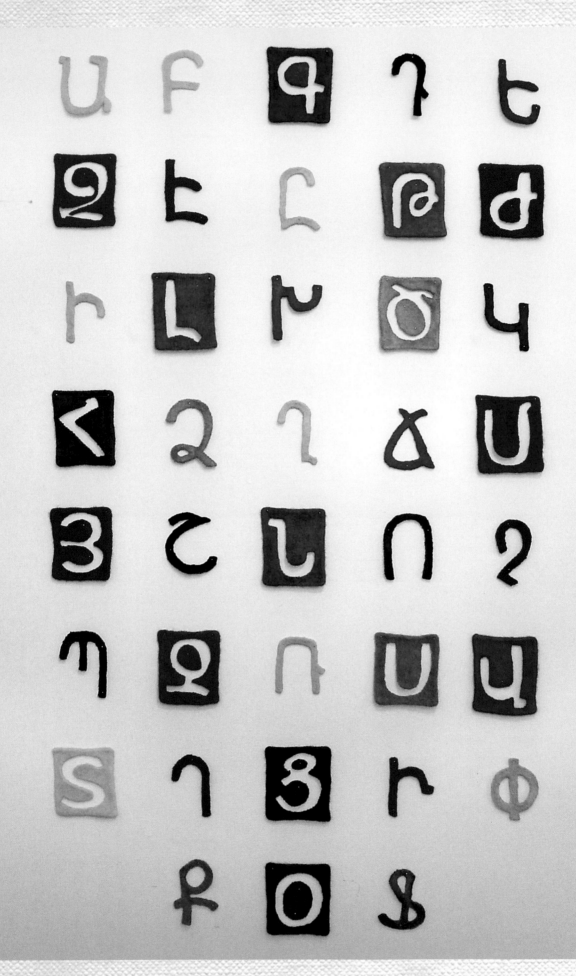

Laura Kamian

Laura Kamian in her studio. *Photograph by Jason McDermott*

Laura Kamian takes a fresh approach to knitting with framed works and installations that emphasize the nature of knitting itself. Educated as a painter, she revisits the styles of 1950s and 1960s abstract modern art, reinventing its forms through textile and women's work. When she learned to knit in 1996, Laura viewed painting as her serious work and knitting as a more leisurely activity, but she felt guilty about having such a judgmental attitude about knitting. Knowing that a different level of technical expertise is required to create a fabric than to adorn its surface, Laura decided to make some knitted work and frame it in a fine art context.

At first she combined the two disciplines, stretching knit pieces over canvases coated with paint and beeswax, and leaving some space between the two surfaces to create shadows. Eventually, the pieces became all knit. "My current work is an attempt to retrain myself in the use of my materials and to redirect my idea of what it means to use them. I try to bring my painterly impulses into balance with the feel of fiber running through my hands. I'm dealing with some of the themes of painting and abstraction, just not dealing with paint anymore. It's easier for me to face the yarn than to face the blank canvas," she admits. By 2000, the focus of Laura's art had shifted from painting to knitting.

Laura has knit 200 squares in different texture and pattern stitches for her *Sampler Series* and arranges them in Mondrian-inspired configurations of lines and rectangles, suggesting architecture. The ends of yarns left hanging down remind her of drips of paint or drawn lines. "Each square contains its own world of information," Laura says. A large grid of 120 squares fills a fifteen-foot-long wall; her smallest configuration consists of eight squares. Even with a small *Sampler* installation, viewers are surprised that there are so many patterns in knitting. They ask, "Is the number of patterns infinite?" Laura would like to think that it is, as she constantly seeks new patterns to try and new colors to mix.

Say the Word, detail of installation | Laura Kamian | 2007 | machine-knit and fulled merino wool, acid dyes

Intrigued by the letter forms of the Armenian alphabet, Laura created this installation of felted wool squares and cut-out letter forms. *Photograph © 2008 by Jeannie O'Connor*

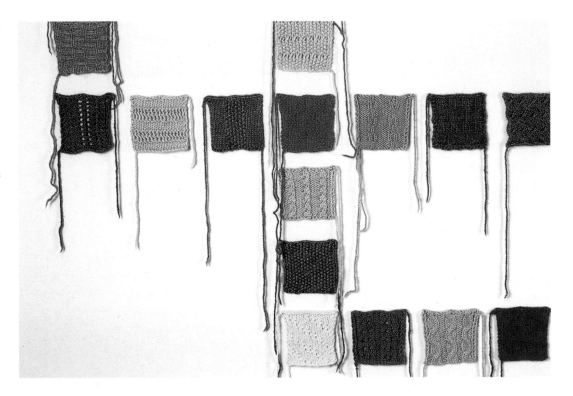

The Sampler Series, detail | Laura Kamian | geometric arrangements of four-inch knitted squares
In her *Sampler Series*, Laura explores the concepts of repetition and endless possible outcomes. She has knit more than 200 squares, each one in a different pattern stitch, for this installation.

Laura prefers grid arrangements for her *Sampler* works because the essential structure of knitting is based on the grid: stitch after stitch, and row upon row. The knitted grid also evokes topics beyond the realm of textiles, such as architecture, digital imaging, painting, and drawing. "My wish is that this *Sampler Series* will reference the 'sameness' or universality of these creative impulses and inspire the idea of infinite possibility within a rigidly structured format. After all, you are looking at 3,640 yards of straight line."

Placing fiber against a white wall highlights its textural and sculptural qualities. Laura's brightly colored three-dimensional "drawings," in the form of lively squiggles and knots in highly saturated colors, suggest gestures or marks in an unknown language. Made of *felted* and dyed *I-cord*, the shrinkage caused by felting creates twists and turns, suggesting their possible arrangements. *Gestures and Knots* consists of cords of varying lengths, from 12 to 244 inches. Some arrangements are large, sweeping gestures similar to brushstrokes, in others the cord twists and tangles itself into knots. In *Alphabets,* Laura arranges small cords to resemble letters. The letters make up words but are arranged randomly, making each arrangement a mysterious phrase to ponder.

Laura is of Armenian descent and visited Armenia for the first time in 2005. Frustrated that she couldn't speak the language, she was also captivated by the beauty of its letterforms and began sketching the Armenian alphabet—first in her sketchbook and later on large sheets of paper covering her studio wall. She then began making felted "stencils" of the letters. She purchased an inexpensive knitting machine to create uniform knitted squares for felting and cut stencil-like letters out of the felted squares. She arranged the positive letter cutouts and the squares together with their negative images on the wall, spelling out words from her family's history. She embellished other plain felted squares with needle felting to create an illuminated manuscript effect. Laura has posted an illustrated journal on her website, www.laurakamian. com, showing the progression of this installation that she calls *Say The Word.* She describes the emotional impact of this work, which was first exhibited in an Oakland, California, gallery in the summer of 2007:

Say The Word begins with a chart of the Armenian alphabet, and from there, a river of letters flows across the four walls, winding through a series of words. The ones I have chosen to spell are taken from my memory of my grandfather's story of survival of the Armenian Genocide in 1915. These words are loaded with the symbolism of his survival: brother, cousin, mother, arsenic, spoon, orphanage, foot, desert, antibiotics. The river that runs through them is symbolic of the river Arax, the root of my grandmother's Americanized name, Roxie. Her spirit joins my

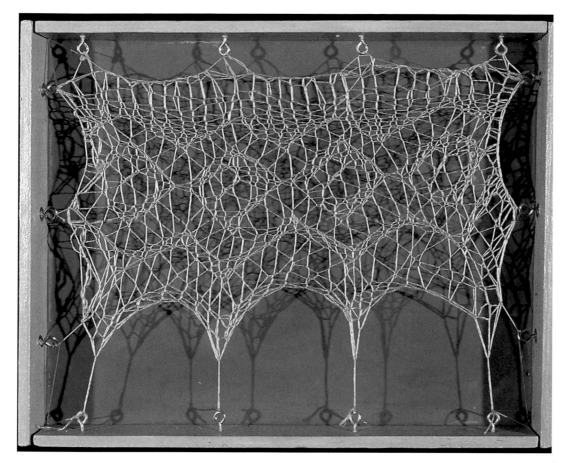

Repeat Pattern | Laura Kamian | 2002 | hand-knit silk lace, oil-and-beeswax painting on masonite | 8" x 10" x 2"

Laura mounted a traditional border pattern knit in an Orenburg lace pattern against a painted background. *Repeat Pattern* was inspired by Galina Khmeleva's *Gossamer Webs Collection.*

grandfather on his treacherous journey, promising hope of a marriage of sixty-plus years and a bright, bustling, and prosperous future together, right here in Oakland, California.

Other recent works include an installation with skeins of yarn and graduated sizes of felted knit swatches. Laura began by making the tiniest swatch and increasing its size by one stitch and one row with each successive swatch. She is also branching out from designing wall-based installations and considering ways to fill a room with knitting.

Laura has considered herself a painter since she was seventeen. She studied weaving, dyeing, and surface design at San Francisco State University and works in the office of Dharma Trading, a distributor of textile painting, printing, and dyeing supplies in San Rafael, California.

She learned to knit while still a college student, when an acquaintance offered to teach her. She caught

on quickly, as knitting's underlying grid structure made perfect sense to her. Her friends were inspired to learn, too, and now they meet for knitting on Sunday mornings. Eventually Laura attended a Stitches conference, where she learned the scribble-knitting technique from Debbie New and used it in some framed works as an abstract landscape. She also attended a class in Orenburg lace, which inspired another framed piece.

The process of knitting is important to Laura, and with each new project she likes to include a new skill to keep pushing herself. She does dyeing and machine knitting in her studio, which is located in an Oakland warehouse, and does the felting at her new home in nearby Richmond.

Laura shares her knowledge with kids in a youth arts program by teaching knitting, dyeing, and felting in Emeryville Secondary School. "I've been told that knitting has changed the culture of the school," she says. "Knitting and exhibiting their work gives the students a sense of accomplishment."

Pink I-cord Gesture |
Laura Kamian | 2006 |
hand-knit, hand-dyed,
and fulled wool I-cord |
38" x 32" x 2"
Laura discovered gestural
qualities in the twistings
and turnings that resulted
from felting her hand-knit
I-cord.

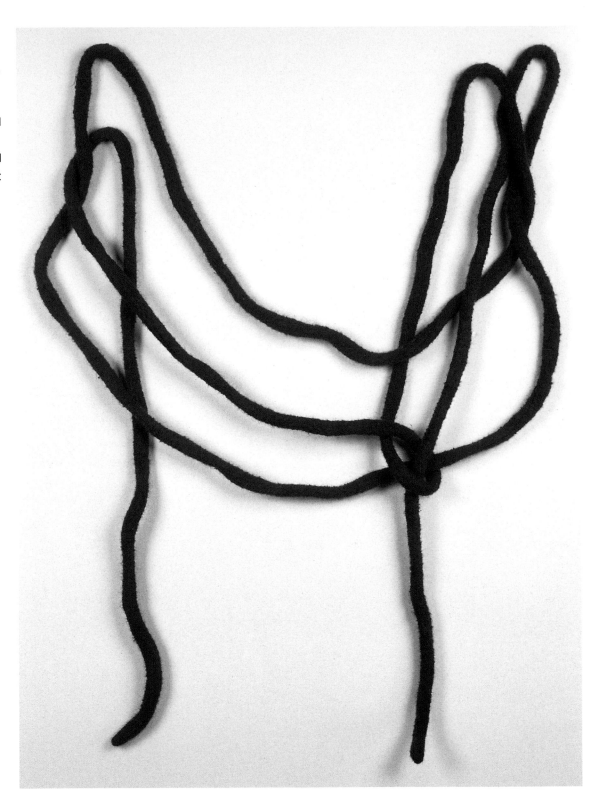

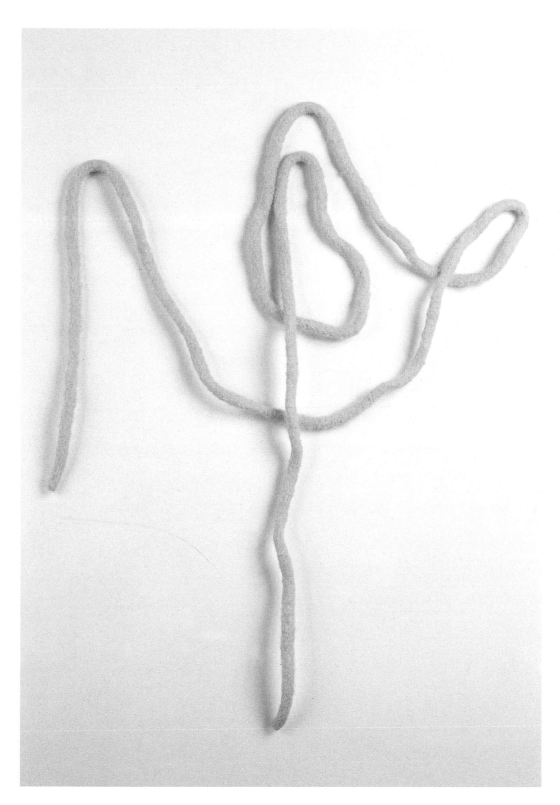

Yellow I-cord Gesture |
Laura Kamian | hand-knit wool, fulled
Once knit, these I-cords are subjected to a rigorous felting process (properly called *fulling*) that shrinks and sets each tube into a permanent, unique gesture. Laura says, "The I-cords tell me how to install them based on the way the fulling process has shrunk and compacted their fibers into definite kinks."

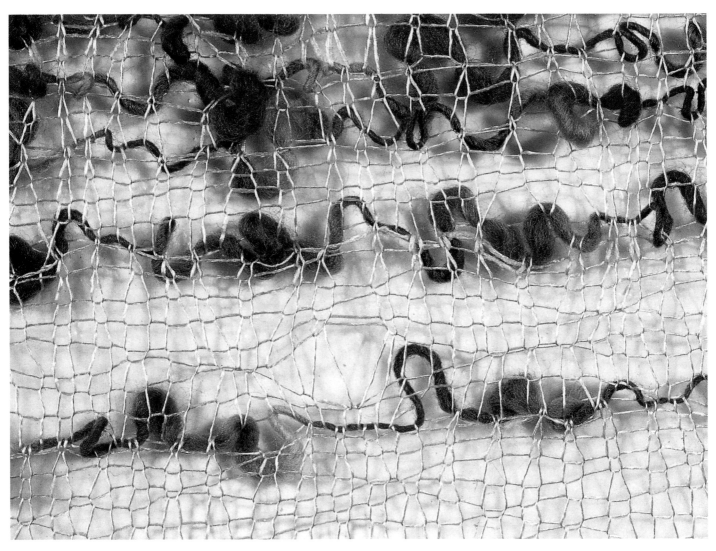

Tension | Laura Kamian | 2002 | hand-knit wool and silk, beeswax on canvas | 23" x 23" x 2"
Laura created a muted shadow effect by placing this delicate knitted web over a painted wax background, which repels the silk. *Tension* was inspired by Debbie New's *Scribble Lace*.

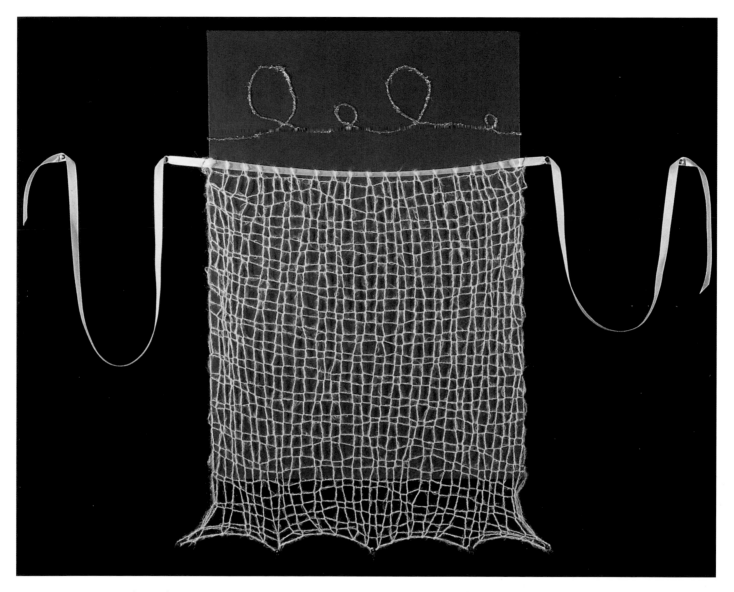

Row 1 | Laura Kamian | 2002 | hand-knit wool, twine, ribbon, acrylic, painted canvas | 39" x 49" x 1"
After making this transitional piece, Laura stopped placing her knitting into a painterly context and began working exclusively with knitting as her medium.

Ilisha Helfman

Ilisha Helfman modeling her *Peacock Shawl* and *Beachcomber Shawl*.

Ilisha Helfman calls herself a "jazz knitter" as she creates magical, dimensional collages through an intuitive knitting process. Curiosity, ingenuity, a sense of humor, and a spirit of adventure all enter into the developing forms and images that emerge from the rainbow of yarn passing through her hands and her needles.

In a process she calls "following the thread—listening carefully to what the yarn has to say, and taking cues from that," Ilisha begins with skeins of fine, hand-painted merino wool and rearranges the dyer's art in unexpected ways. Using garter stitch and size zero needles, she skillfully works with *short rows*, following the dyer's spontaneous color choices and changing the direction of her knitting with each shift of the yarn's color.

As a young designer, Ilisha produced hand-printed textile designs. She would challenge herself to see how many variations she could make from the same printing block, then alter the block slightly to evolve the design. She has applied this designer's mode of thinking to her freestyle knitting process by setting basic ground rules for herself. She chooses one hue in the multicolor skein as her base color and knits a small shape with it. As the color shifts into a new hue, she "pools" the new color with short rows; as the yarn shifts back to the original hue, she tapers the emerging shape to join it with the original color area. The form evolves along with the color changes in unexpected ways as Ilisha lets her ideas evolve along with the form.

"I was surprised at what would happen as I adhered to those rules," she says. "Each piece was a discovery of a new shape or form. Gingko leaves led to peacocks, peacock tails led to ruffling, which led to sea lettuces and other sea forms. Follow the thread—watch what happens. I might think I'm making a sea lettuce or a spotlight, but it turns into a bird! If I start with an idea in mind, I don't stick to it—if it wants to be something else, I let it."

Forest 1 | Ilisha Helfman | 2004 | hand-knit variegated merino wool
Ilisha used her "following the thread" or "jazz knitting" process to create this group of leaf, flower, mushroom, and insect-like forms, which she can use as elements in a collage.

Gingko Leaves | Ilisha Helfman | 2004 | hand-knit variegated merino wool
Ilisha, who calls herself a "jazz knitter," produced a group of colorful leaf shapes and attached them to an I-cord to create a decorative scarf/necklace.

Each variable in Ilisha's basic rule set yields a different type of shape or form. Differing dye effects in the skein of yarn provide one variable. A second variable is her choice of the color to "collect" inside the form and the color she places at the edges. She discovered that slight alterations to the rule set added dimensionality: for instance, seashell shapes emerged with the addition of pattern stitches, increases, and decreases. Because she works the curved shapes on straight needles, Ilisha often discovers surprising twists and curls when the needles are removed, adding an energetic dimensional element to the knitted forms.

Once Ilisha amasses a collection of exotic shapes and forms, she arranges and rearranges them into collages or uses them as motifs for trimming shawls and garments. One group of collages features leaves and fungi, another suggests ocean life forms. In a third series of collages, she strove to create figurative forms and, recalling time spent in art history lectures, arranged them in compositions that make oblique references to famous sculptures and paintings.

To mount her figurative collages for exhibition, Ilisha knit some gossamer backgrounds in clear monofilament with seed beads and stretched them over acid-free boards. Her shapes and forms float on the sparkling surfaces, casting shadows that add further dimensionality to the works. "The beaded nets on which these images are collaged are a fond look back to the sparkling lunch-lady hairnets of my youth," she quips.

Ilisha paints with watercolors and enjoys the way the hand-painted yarn is a saturated line of color, like a painted line on paper. "I like the challenge of using a line that's already painted to make imagery," she says. "It's a nice complement to painting, where I create the lines of color while looking at an image for inspiration."

Ilisha lives in northwest Connecticut and is the mother of two teenagers. She received her MFA in Graphic Design from Yale University and is an award-winning graphic designer, often collaborating on projects with her equally inventive designer husband, Joe Freedman. She also creates miniature objects for dollhouses and collectors through her business Hestia House, selling her work online at www.hestiahouse.com and at international miniature shows.

She is the daughter of professional artists: her mother was a tapestry artist and her father is a watercolorist. "I guess growing up surrounded by the creation of tapestries by my mother and her

Nude Sunbathing, After Miró | Ilisha Helfman | hand-knit variegated merino wool, monofilament, glass beads | 4-½" x 4-½"
Ilisha knit individual abstract motifs, "following the thread" and using short rows to control the placement of color areas when using a variegated skein of yarn. This arrangement of motifs reminded her of a Miró painting, and she mounted it on a knitted background of monofilament with beads.

Water Dress | Ilisha Helfman | 1981 | hand-knit variegated merino wool
This elegant garment was Ilisha's first experiment in "following the thread"—using short rows to control color placement with variegated yarn.

apprentices, it's natural for me see imagery in fiber," Ilisha says. "While my brother and I literally grew up under our mother's loom, doing homework and watching TV and making things, it's hard to really be with a person who is weaving. I like that I can sit next to others while I knit, and I like how I can carry it around with me—something my mother could never do."

Ilisha works her garter stitch pieces from the front side whenever possible, usually in purling, her preferred technique. As a very young knitter, she imitated her mother, who always wove her tapestry designs from the front side of the fabric. Thinking of her stockinette-stitch fabric in the same way, Ilisha acquired the habit of knitting across from right to left, then knitting back from left to right—changing hands rather than turning the piece—so she would always see the front of her work.

Some of Ilisha's art works on paper are dimensional collages using mixed print ephemera with fabric piecing. She immediately saw the possibilities for a new type of collage in her knitted experiments. "I have always had an open mind when it comes to collage and have combined textiles and collage in different ways," she explains. She has applied her designer's mind and a similar freestyle knitting process to an exciting series of garments using Noro variegated yarn and evolving the design slightly with each new garment. She calls the collection *Triple Noro*, and has published a pattern book and created a website (www.triplenoro.com) where she shows images of the garments, explains the rules she followed in her design process, and distributes her pattern books and kits. Another portion of the site contains images of her "following the thread" art works.

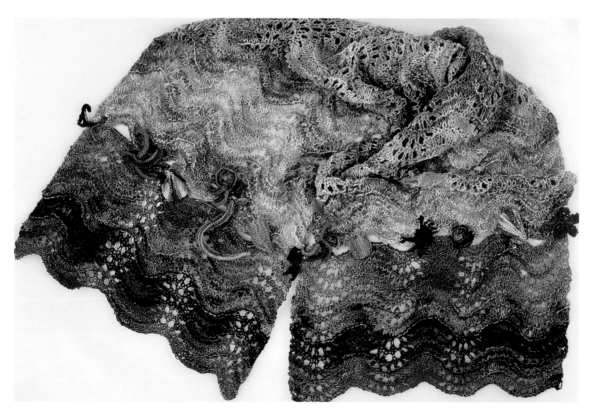

Beachcomber Shawl |
Ilisha Helfman |
2004 | hand-knit
variegated merino
wool with knitted
embellishments
Some of Ilisha's
experiments in "following
the thread" produced
abstract shapes
reminiscent of seashells,
sea cucumbers, and sea
lettuces. Ilisha adorned
her ocean-blue lace
shawl with these forms.

Reclining Nude, After Schiele | Ilisha Helfman | 2006 | hand-knit variegated merino wool, monofilament, glass beads | 8-¼" x 8-½"
Ilisha knit the bead-embellished individual motifs and composed them into a collage that reminded her of a painting by Egon Schiele. She mounted the collage on a knit background of monofilament with beads.

Water Nymph, After Goujon | Ilisha Helfman | 2006 |
hand-knit variegated merino wool, monofilament, glass
beads | 15-½" x 6"
Ilisha creates many individual motifs for her collages. For this one
she selected seaweed-like forms to arrange with a female figure
in a composition that reminds her of a sculpture by Goujon. The
collage is mounted on a knitted background of monofilament
with beads.

Debbie New

It wasn't until Debbie New had reached her fifties that she set out to see for herself what can be done with knitting. By applying her scientifically trained mind, her natural curiosity, and her innate sense of color and harmony, Debbie has opened many new frontiers for knitters. Her book *Unexpected Knitting* outlines her unorthodox approaches to making garments, objects, and art. Debbie finds knitting to be "intellectually engaging and mind-expanding," adding, "I'm conscious that this is a soft medium and that I'm doing something that's unexpected."

A musician and scientist as well as a knitter, Debbie recently challenged herself to combine music and knitting by incorporating concepts of time and movement into interactive knitted sculptures. "It's not easy to combine a linear medium, such as music, with the visual, which is immediate," she explains. An early music-related piece, *Duet for Thread and Theremin* initiated this line of thought. "Rather whistly" sounds emanate from a theremin as the viewer pulls on projections in the knitted piece mounted above it. Naturally, Debbie also built the theramin. "This piece took off from two ideas coming together from different disciplines," she says. "And because knitting is so slow, it gives you lots more ideas while you're making it."

Her functioning *Knitted Clock* was an early attempt to make a kinetic knitted work. *Ten Ugly Hats* is a recent interactive piece based on kaleidoscopic effects. As Debbie describes it, "They are ten identical hats, individually ugly, arranged in mirror-image pairs. When they are in a symmetrical array, they become beautiful because of the symmetry, and when whirling around, they are like a kaleidoscope." *The Eye of the Beholder* is about finding interest or beauty in any situation. Its designs are ever-changing as the viewer's position and angle of view changes. Although Debbie easily accomplishes the knitting portion of these works, it takes time and trial and error to work out their technical aspects.

Debbie New at work knitting the panels of her installation, *Labyrinth of Rebirth*. The large needles were made specially for her by a boat builder in England.

Labyrinth of Rebirth | Debbie New | 2001 | hand-knit mohair, aluminum | 20' x 12' x 7' tall
Debbie knit thirty-three mohair panels, which she mounted on gazebo frames and arranged into a walk-through labyrinth. She used symbols of fetal development as imagery on some of the outer panels.
Photographs by Sandy Nicholson

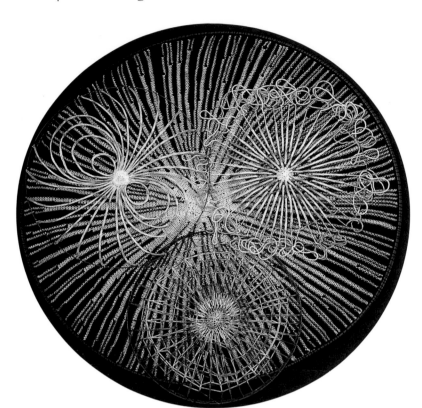

Close-up detail, one plane of *Eye of the Beholder*.

Eye of the Beholder | Debbie New | 2007 | hand-knit yarns and metallic threads
Debbie's latest innovative knitted work is comprised of a complex assemblage of knitted pieces hanging so that they interact with each other as you walk past. Its appearance changes as the viewer's position changes, making it impossible to capture its full effect in a photograph.

Debbie grew up in Australia, where, she insists, "you were born knowing how to knit." In primary school, students were required to make knitted items for donation to a charity, "but nobody taught us knitting at school, because it was assumed that everybody could knit." It was when Debbie was in primary school that she recalls her mother teaching her to follow patterns.

Debbie has a microbiology degree and also studied art and music. She has lived in Australia, England, and Canada, and currently resides near Toronto. Her various careers have included microbiological research, biomedical engineering, teaching, symphony violinist, and potter—all coinciding with roles as wife, mother, grandmother, and caregiver. When her husband became disabled, she dropped out of work to care for him. By that time, most of her brood of eight kids were grown, so she had the freedom to approach her knitting with a sense of adventure and to explore without needing to think about functionality. Since she knew nothing of fiber arts, she found a local knitter's guild and attended a few workshops. Her first nonfunctional workshop-inspired project was a knitted teacup and

saucer made in 1993. "I wanted to make something freestanding that just used the shape of knitting to hold itself up," she says.

Debbie designs as she works, feeling that if she plans out a piece in every detail, the knitting part becomes merely an exercise. "You have to do that if you are writing patterns, but having it all set in stone before you start is not the way I really like to work. I'd rather have something where you knit a bit and then see what you want to do with it—creating as you go." She developed an adaptation of *freeform knitting* to satisfy this creative tendency.

A unique group of clothing designs she calls "swirl knitting," based on knitting circles and arcs, came from exploring the nature of knitting and from asking, "Must knitting always be in straight lines?" Her "Ouroboros" knitting technique came from asking, "How can I make something circular that doesn't need cutting?" She developed an Ouroboros-style jacket design that was quite complex. "After that I thought, 'How can this be simplified so that others can do it?' I simplified it down and down until I had a baby sweater with the instructions being only one row long! For me that's quite pleasing—that I can get it that

Brain Hat | Debbie New | hand-knit cottons | from the collection of Charlotte Quiggle
The idea for *Brain Hat* came to Debbie when she saw brain coral while snorkeling on the Great Barrier Reef in Australia.

Ten Ugly Hats | Debbie New | 2007 | hand-knit Shetland wool, wood base, metal mountings, gears, and cranks
In Debbie's revolutionary kinetic sculpture, ten conical hats knitted in Fair-Isle patterns are mounted in a mechanized frame. When a crank is turned, each pair of cones turns in opposite directions, and a series of kaleidoscopic images is produced. It took Debbie several months to work out the mechanics of this piece.

simple. Then, having done that, while I'm working on these things slowly, I think, 'Why couldn't I do it that way?' And I complicate it again."

Further research on constructing one-piece, garter-stitch garments led to a labyrinth sweater design made from a single, long, mitered garter-stitch strip that must be laid out correctly to form the garment. The design was originally conceived as a puzzle for her grandchildren to solve.

"Rule-generated patterns" developed after Debbie knit some shell sculptures and realized that shells are fractals. She became interested in generating fractals as forms. Her scientifically minded filmmaker son suggested looking at cellular automata, a term used in physics to describe snowflake patterns, and she found it to be "quite fun. If you translate it into knitting, each stitch is made according to what is already in place, and that generates a pattern," she explains.

Mathematician Daina Taimina's crocheted planes led to Debbie's experiments with knitting hyperbolic plane forms, as in her *Hyperbolic Hat*.

Debbie has created numerous sculptures as well as some large works and installations. *Labyrinth of Rebirth* consists of thirty-three panels—a total of 450 square feet of knitting—which can be erected in many configurations. Her 10-foot-tall *Granny Squares* was made by dividing a picture of her grandmother into square units and rendering each unit in garter-stitch log-cabin blocks. One of Debbie's most unique accomplishments was to knit a seaworthy coracle, a small round boat dating from prehistoric times and still in use in British waterways.

Debbie's work is based on not predicting outcomes but keeping a sense of curiosity and wonder, even to the extent of including puns, jests, and curiosities. As she explains her working process, "It needs to have some interest for me to make something, and sometimes it's a structural thing, like a circle or a labyrinth. Sometimes the challenge is in the color or shape, or it may come from another field entirely. It's rare that I use patterns, so I don't get to learn about what others have discovered—I am often inventing

Peacock Coat | Debbie New | 1997 | knitted mohair lined with chiffon
Knitted medallions and strips of swirl knitting comprise the shaped design of this coat. Debbie originally wanted to restrict herself to using peacock colors, but her favorite warm colors snuck into the mix. *Photograph by Sandy Nicholson*

things that other people already know. That's all right, though. I like inventing things."

Debbie comes out of a tradition where knitting was women's work and doesn't resist that label. She calls herself "knitter" rather than "artist," feeling that as an artist, she would have to limit herself. "It should be a free thing, but I feel that I would have to have identifiable works and be relevant to my century, and so on. Or I would always have to knit something that's making a statement—I couldn't just sit down and knit

a pair of socks, even if I felt like it. Where as a knitter, I can do what I feel like."

Debbie has taught many workshops in Canada, the United States, Australia, and Europe. Her book summarizes her teaching. She always asks herself and her readers, "where else can you take this idea?" and offers one or two possibilities to spur their thinking. "I could have worked in any medium," she muses. "I decided to see what I could do with knitting. It hasn't run out, yet."

Granny Squares |
Debbie New | hand-knit natural wool and alpaca | 10' x 7'
To honor the skills passed down from generation to generation, Debbie enlarged a picture of her grandmother, divided it into square units, and knit them as garter-stitch log-cabin blocks. The blocks were crocheted together and stitched to a backing.
Photograph by Sandy Nicholson

Knitted Lace Coracle | Debbie New | 1999 | hand-knit merino wool and crochet cotton
One of Debbie's sons holds her knitted lace coracle, a sailing vessel as well as a work of art. Ancient coracles were made by stretching hides over a wood framework and sealing them with lanolin or tar. Debbie's seaworthy coracle is sealed with fiberglass resin. *Photograph by Sandy Nicholson*

Pebbles Trapped in a Grate |
Debbie New | 1994 |
mixed fibers and
padding | 3' x 4'
This knit vignette with
stones was inspired by a
photo of pebbles taken by
Debbie's daughter-in-law,
who was active in Amnesty
International.

Katharine Cobey

Katharine Cobey

Artist, poet, and outspoken feminist Katharine Cobey boldly investigates knitting's unlimited potential for expression, busily showing the world that "knitting can grow up." Turning a thread into a three-dimensional symbolic construction has occupied her creative muse ever since she realized that she could create visual metaphors with her knitting needles. She speaks in her work about dress, ritual, myth, shelter, promise, pretense, grief, hope, and life.

Katharine has been an emissary for art knitting through her exhibitions and her teaching. Direct, honest, inventive, passionate, opinionated, adamant, and critical, her conversation is punctuated with exclamations. "Knitting is a three-dimensional technique," she explains. "We have been ignoring half of what knitting can do by focusing on making fabric. Knitting is organic, sensual, and full of possibilities. Understanding its structure, using our minds, and observing what is happening with the work will move the artform forward."

A lifelong feminist, Katharine urges knitters to use the medium expressively to elevate it from its domestic identification. "After nine hundred years or so, it is time for us to enter an age of mature work," she opines. "We need to knit with more than just the sweet side of us." She is critical of the "just follow the directions" mindset, which she considers a related feminist issue—that of being "good girls"—and encourages knitters to think about what they are doing, take themselves seriously, and create works of significance. "We can't do that if we devalue ourselves and our work."

Katharine takes a sculptural approach to knitting, using basic stitches and taking advantage of how each fiber behaves. An accomplished spinner, she often creates her own yarns, or she may use found materials for the symbolism she finds in them, which is usually sparked by a deep emotional response. During the first Gulf

Danger Dress | Katharine Cobey | 1996 | hand-cut, hand-knit black plastic and construction-site tape dress and mobile | 53" x 24" x 15"
Katharine enjoys the visual pun in the skirt of this attractive formal dress made from recycled plastics.

Dream Shelters, installation with five figures | Katharine Cobey | 1990 | handspun, hand-knit wool, found wood, fossil shells, timbers | 15' h x 12' w x 25' l

Dream Shelters was Katharine's first installation work in knitting. It consists of four blankets, a coat, a cape, and a shawl arranged on a bed of antique oyster shells. Katharine recalls, "When we were kids, we built shelters and teepees from a trunk of dress-up stuff." *Photograph by David Boyce Cobey*

War, she cut up black plastic trash bags—a petroleum product—to knit a work expressing her grief over the "collateral damage" caused when birds became trapped in the oil spill issuing from a destroyed tanker.

Katharine thinks big. Many of her works are large-scale installations requiring the construction of an armature or scaffolding to support them, and she may also incorporate found objects. Often there is a ceremonial aspect, such as in the circle of figures that comprises *Ritual Against Homelessness* or the thirty-foot-long *Boat with Four Figures* that was six years in the making. Inspired by watching a small boat on the Potomac River, she created an ode to moving forward that incorporates her feelings about making art, making friendships, and making a life.

In *The Pillars*, Katharine has embarked on her largest project to date in homage to the feminine spirit. She has completed two out of a planned set of twelve eight-foot-tall Greek-style columns knitted of handspun wool. When they are all completed, they will comprise an installation called *Making Room*. Katharine was moved to create this work when she saw relationships between Greek architectural columns, the design and drape of a Greek Peplos, and the ancient groves of trees where people worshipped before temples were built.

Katharine, who proudly owns up to being seventy-years young, lives with her husband, David, in an old farmhouse in an idyllic setting overlooking the tidal Mundoocook River on the Maine coast. In the beautiful studio David built for her, the dramatic and moving *Ritual Against Homelessness* fills the gallery area, and many knitted artworks cover the walls. A group of *diagonally knitted* works-in-process hangs from the rafters, twisting and spiraling in the air. She grew excited about their sculptural potential. "We haven't discovered all the possibilities in knitting yet—at all! It is absolutely fascinating."

Katharine can recall herself knitting at age eleven. Although her mother could knit, Katharine's left-handedness and dyslexia required the patient teaching of a willing neighbor. "I never really stopped knitting after that," she says, "though often I couldn't afford the yarn it was a luxury." She was raised in an intellectual New England family and educated at Bennington College. She recalls encountering disparaging attitudes toward knitting in those environments.

Although she enjoyed knitting, it remained a hobby during the years she was a wife and mother who also enjoyed a successful career as a poet.

While recovering from a back injury in 1986, knitting's expressive qualities revealed themselves to Katharine. Initially a physical activity that she could manage to do while recovering, knitting became a great pleasure, and her explorations of visual metaphors began to overshadow her interest in evoking images with words. She felt challenged to accomplish through knitting everything she could do with poetry, and more. "Craft is interesting—the thingness of it," Katharine muses. "Painters represent a coat. I'm making the coat, and I make it speak. I like its thingness very much." Although she no longer creates verbal poetry, she is knitting visual poetry, and our lives are enriched by her choice of needles and yarn over pen and paper.

Looking back on this period of discovery and the choice to knit her art, Katharine wonders, "What was I thinking? I didn't know anybody who had done anything like this—I knew nothing about fiber artists. You just have gall sometimes!" She quickly found that it was much easier to be taken seriously as a female poet than as a sculptor who knits, and she disparages the constant need to defend her choice of artistic medium. "I am making things by knitting that I believe to be art. They signify something to me and to others," she states. Katharine is not fond of looking at works that lack meaning—"make it mean something!" she shouts. "Skill alone does not make a knitted object 'speak.' The whole piece must be permeated by the meaning you intend."

Katharine is a popular teacher, traveling annually to present workshops in summer arts programs. Currently she is taking time out from her artwork to write a book on diagonal knitting for Schoolhouse Press, and she looks forward to the time when she can allow her artistic muse to run free again.

Reflecting on her past work, Katharine realized that she has produced more than 1,600 objects so far, many of which are pictured on her new website, www.katharinecobey.com. "When you're in the process of making one thing, you're always thinking ,'What else?' It stirs you up. You put everything you have into your work—but you can't put it all into one piece! That's what keeps us going as artists."

Mime for the Gulf War Birds, standing figure | Katharine Cobey | 1994 | hand-cut, hand-knit black plastic on wood base | 6' h x 3' w x 3' d During the first Gulf War, Katharine was especially moved by the plight of birds trapped in an oil spill and used black trash bags, made from petroleum products, for this elegy. *Photograph by David Boyce Cobey*

Left and below:

Boat with Four Figures,
installation | Katharine Cobey
| 1999 | handspun, hand-knit
wool with stainless steel
cables and supports |
6' h x 30' l x 12' w
A spectral boat moves on, across
geography and through time,
containing figures representing
anonymous women. Katharine
spent five years spinning the wool
and knitting the two sixty-foot-
long, five-foot-wide, gray mohair
panels of this installation (in
garter stitch on size 11 needles).
One panel forms the boat and
its wake; the other drapes like a
shroud over four crude wooden
figures carved by Katharine from
spruce logs that she harvested
from her land. She learned
woodcarving in order to render
the figures. *Photograph by David
Boyce Cobey*

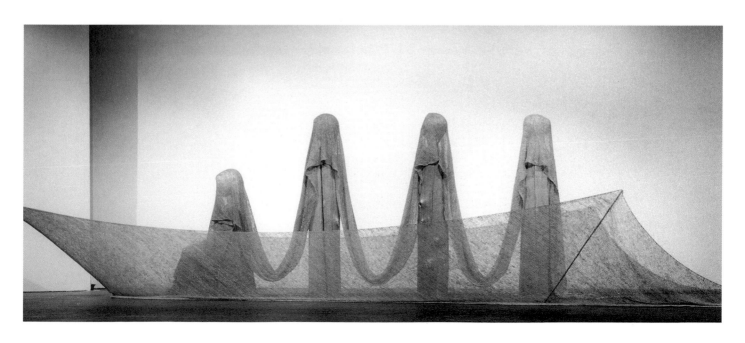

Ritual Against Homelessness, installation detail | Katharine Cobey |1992 | handspun hand-knit Churro wool, leather, shell, bone
Katharine presents a circle of personages represented by their empty tunics in this moving outdoor installation. *Photograph by David Boyce Cobey*

Pillars | Katharine Cobey | 2008 | handspun, hand-knit wool, acrylic hanger | 7-10' ¾" h x 2' diameter at base

This installation work-in-process will eventually consist of twelve Greek-style pillars knit by Katharine in homage to ancient outdoor sites of worship. Like her *Boat with Four Figures*, it will take Katharine several years to complete this work. *Photograph by David Boyce Cobey*

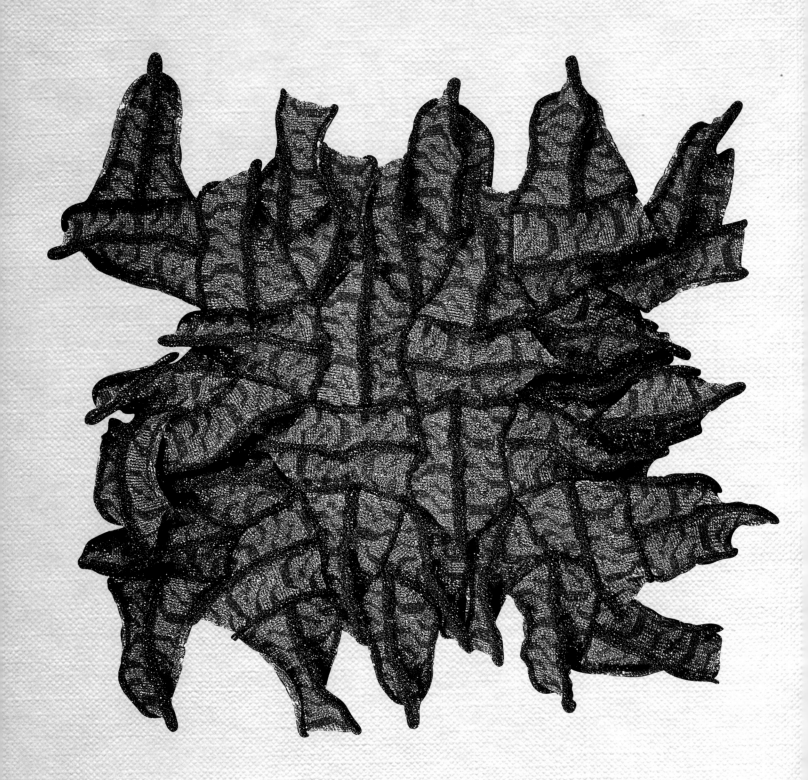

Donna L. Lish

Donna Lish knitting in
her backyard.

"Follow no rules!" summarizes the approach Donna Lish has taken to knitting
works of art by machine and by hand since the 1980s. Working with light-reflective
materials, she explores the intersection of interior and exterior space in both
large installations and small, intimate sculptures. Her process is intuitive and
experiential, melding fresh contexts and technologically produced materials with
techniques and stitches that are steeped in tradition.

It seems that knitting her art was a "given" for Donna. She recalls a time when
she was seven: while her mother was knitting, she noticed her daughter's hands
moving in imitation. "She put knitting needles into my hands and started me
off," Donna says. She learned to crochet from her grandmother and soon became
comfortable using both techniques. Occasional attempts at garment-making proved
frustrating, however, until she discovered the knitting machine in 1985. Realizing
that the machine would let her pursue both her love of knitting and her love of
making sculpture, she made the purchase.

In an early project, she used materials that were unsuitable for the machine and
tore the piece off in frustration. "That was actually my biggest discovery!" Donna
exclaimed. "It looked like a splash of water or a sea of raindrops, the way the fibers
undulated and picked up the light, and I took off with that." Her series of large wall
pieces with water imagery and the effects of light meandering across the surfaces
were shown in the prestigious Lausanne Biennale de Tapisserie in 1987, launching
a long career of showing her work in national and international exhibitions and
receiving many honors.

Intrigued by form, Donna continues to explore sculptural possibilities on
the machine, adding handknitting, crochet, or beading as the emerging structure
requires. She is intrigued by light-reflective materials that convey a sense of

Mumbo-Jumble | Donna L. Lish | machine-knitted monofilament and estralin with hand
stitching | 38" tall x 45" wide x 5" deep
Donna created this large work by knitting small modular units and then stitching them together. She trimmed
the seams with beading to add both a decorative element and structural support. *Photograph by Peter Jacobs*

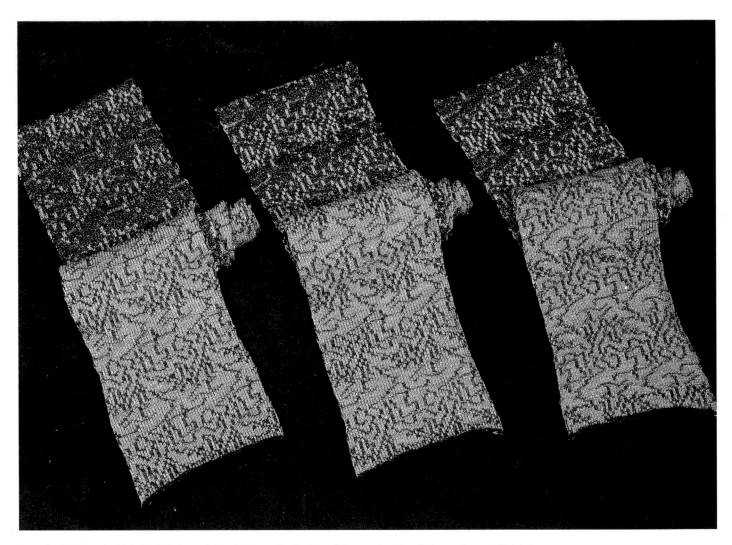

Scrolls | Donna L. Lish | 2006 | machine-knit synthetic fiber | 3 panels 9" x 25", center roll 8" high
From Donna's series of knitted "books." She designed a text-like pattern card for her knitting machine to create an impression of ancient writings in her scroll installation. *Photograph by Peter Jacobs*

the spiritual, and she follows a complex process of selecting the appropriate materials for carrying out her imagery. "It's an abstracted and emotionally charged way of working and attaining my sense of vision and form," she says. Her works are based on initial research, which inspires the conceptual execution, including any symbolic and technical considerations.

For Donna, knitting and her stream of consciousness are closely allied. She is an avid reader, especially in the fields of philosophy and psychology. As she works, her readings spark thoughts and reflections that she relates to the linear elements in her hands and to the emerging form. "The stream of consciousness and the stitching that mimics it in a cellular construction are integral to my work," she explains. "The result is very cohesive with my temperament and whatever intrigues me at the time,

and whatever goes into the research behind it, which is always changing."

Donna begins with a completed image in mind, refining it internally before actually beginning the piece, which continues to evolve as she works. Before she starts, she asks many questions: What will happen if I use this as a foundation? How is that stitch going to withstand stretching? How will the weight of the piece be held if I suspend it? Does it need to be supported from within? "It's a continual enrichment," she says. "I am learning and solving problems constantly—the fibers' tendency to twist and curl, a bulge that you didn't expect—fiber allows me to alter my approach as the complexities evolve. That's what we do as artists—we solve problems that lead us to something else, and then we meander from there . . ."

Floating Free of Time | Donna L. Lish | 2007 | hand-knit synthetic fiber, glass beads, 6' h x 4' w x 4' d
This two-part installation is mostly handknit. Donna's silvery forms recline in the air, suggesting repose. *Photograph by Peter Jacobs*

Some recent installations consist of large-scale "shards of light" suspended above large container forms. A group of small, two-layer works called *Channels and Openings* explores light-reflective materials and layering. Her Colony series and her Tunnels and Chambers series were inspired by the structures that house ants. *Floating Free of Time* is part of a series of mostly hand-knit, spontaneous sculptures with beaded accents and crochet added for rigidity. Her large Book installations are demanding works, requiring precise preplanning. They are machine-knitted and handstitched together or joined together on the machine. Donna's work is displayed on her website, www.libeado-designs.com.

Donna's engineering turn of mind likes to devise ways to incorporate a piece's foundation or support into the knitting process; or to deal with edges, which sometimes don't turn out neatly. One edge solution

for pieces constructed of modular units involved adding beading to both join the edges and provide an exoskeleton of support. For another creative edge solution, Donna worked the beginning and ending rows of each modular unit in a looser material. In the finished piece, those softer areas could be tucked over the edges to form a binding.

It is hard to imagine works of such scale and complexity taking form in Donna's tiny home studio in Clinton, New Jersey, which barely accommodates her knitting machine. She must constantly strive to be organized and efficient in her working processes to make the best use of the space. She punches her own designs into the program cards for her older-model machine, inventing pattern motifs such as those resembling text in her books and scrolls. Sometimes she has to adapt the machine to handle the many strands of metallic and synthetic materials that are

Transfusion installation | Donna L. Lish | 2005 | hand-knit surgical tubing, crochet, and beading | 7' h x 2' w x 2' d A lucky "find" of surgical tubing inspired Donna to make this piece. *Photograph by Peter Jacobs*

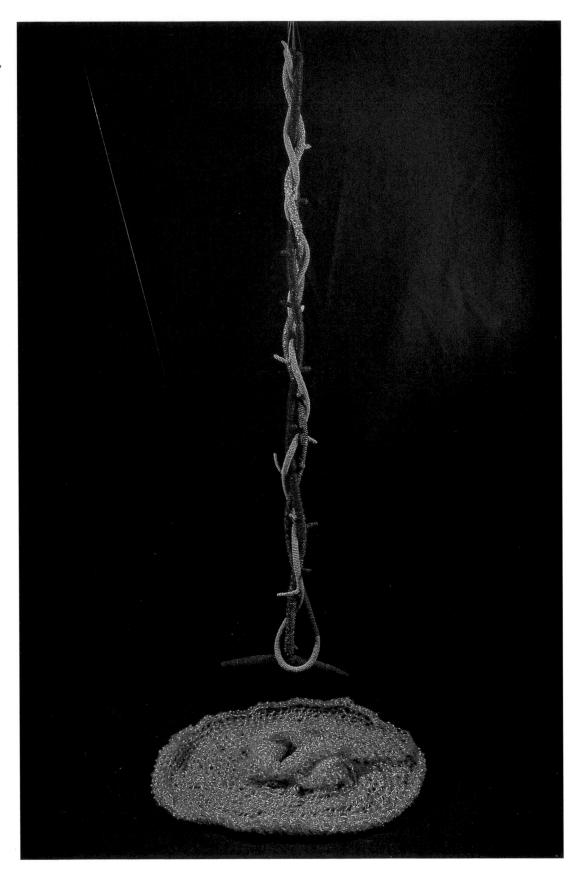

Ascent | Donna L. Lish | machine-knit monofilament, metallic thread, stitching, beading | 53" x 70" x 3" deep
Donna was seeking depth in this series of large knitted wall works and accomplished it by knitting modular units, which she could manipulate and assemble. She designed the surface pattern and had to adapt her knitting machine in order to feed in the numerous strands of fibers. *Photograph by Peter Jacobs*

fed into it. She works on several projects at once, in various scales, in part to help prevent repetitive motion injuries. She usually has a machine-knit piece, a hand-knit piece, and a crochet or bead piece in process at any given time.

A lifelong New Jersey resident, Donna holds bachelor and master's degrees in art education from Montclair State University, New Jersey, and a doctorate in education from Rutgers University. She has enjoyed a rich thirty-year career as a K–12 art teacher and teaching evening or weekend knitting classes at the Hunterdon Museum in Clinton. She and her husband, who is also a teacher, have raised three children. Since Donna's retirement in 2003, she is free to travel, teach workshops, and concentrate full-time on developing new work.

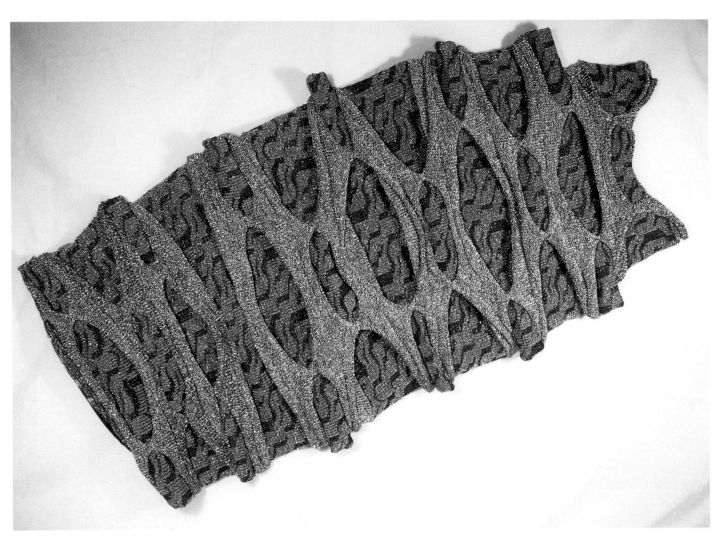

Midday Ripple | Donna L. Lish | machine-knit metallic threads | 38" tall x 20" wide x 2" deep
This piece is part of Donna's *Channels and Openings* series. The pieces are constructed of two knitted layers: the background is patterned and the top layer has slits, allowing the background to show through. *Photograph by Peter Jacobs*

Spectra | Donna L. Lish | 2007 | synthetic fiber, hand-knit and crochet | 19" h x 8" w x 8" d
Donna's *Spectra* series of basket/container forms combine handknitting and crochet, sometimes with beaded embellishments.
Photograph by Peter Jacobs

Lindsay Obermeyer

Lindsay Obermeyer at work on her public sculpture *Adjust the Thermostat.*

Textiles, especially knitted ones, and the ties of motherhood are central to the art of Lindsay Obermeyer. Her sweater sculptures are iconic, drop-shoulder, garment forms in stockinette stitch, made with lipstick shades of good-quality yarns. Her performances embrace knitting as a visual metaphor for our interconnectedness as humans. Lindsay says of her work, "The enduring connection of textiles to the body offers rich metaphorical possibilities for exploring the idea of identity as we attempt to integrate our inner psychic reality with the outside world and make sense of the experience of living."

A native of St. Louis, Missouri, Lindsay is well-known for her embroidery and beadwork. She received her BFA degree from the Art Institute of Chicago. After studying embroidery at Goldsmith's College/University of London, Lindsay received her MFA from the University of Washington. She returned to Chicago and purchased a yarn shop in 1994. In short order, she added knitting to her artist's vocabulary. She finds the repetitive process of knitting important, both in clearing her mind and in connecting to herself and to her visual perspective on the world. Knitting's social aspects provide a welcome balance to her solitary studio work with beads and thread. "Working on my knitting in public places never fails to spark interesting conversations and often a mutual admiration of projects," she explains.

In 1995, on becoming the adoptive mother of seven-year-old Emily, an emotionally challenged Romanian girl, Lindsay began using knitting to explore and express the tremendous elasticity of the mother-child bond. "Like a knitted garment, this bond can stretch, rip, fray, or unravel as the child grows and matures. It is in a perpetual cycle of mending and loosening until death creates the final separation." Faced with a difficult initial adjustment period, Lindsay instinctively understood that hand-knit sweaters would calm the frightened girl and quickly produced a mother/daughter sweater set connected by fifteen-foot-long sleeves.

Weighed Down | Lindsay Obermeyer | 2005 | hand-knit mohair | 20" x 19"
This sweater sculpture is part of Lindsay's *Woman's Work* series, which examines aspects of motherhood.
Photograph by Larry Sanders

Red Thread Project | Lindsay Obermeyer | Grand Rapids | 2006
Lindsay checks the arrangement of hand-knit hats connected by lengths of red I-cord before the start of a performance in Grand Rapids, Michigan.
Volunteers donned the hats and experienced their connection with others physically and visually while performing choreographed movements
together. After the performance, the cords were removed and the hats were donated to charity.

The sleeves' stretchability allowed Emily the freedom to explore her new world, while feeling the physical reassurance of a maternal presence, even when Lindsay was out of sight. A few years later, in the performance, *Connection*, mother and daughter walked through Chicago's Loop in this garment, interacting with the people they met.

Another body of work grew out of Lindsay's new role as a single parent. "My *Woman's Work* series speaks to the need to find a balance between work and children. Once I became a parent, I could no longer spend long tracks of time at my embroidery table. Teaching, trips to the doctor, basketball practice, music lessons, etc. pulled me in a zillion directions a day. Rather than let the stress overwhelm me, I found a way to make art that allowed me to juggle all the other demands." She began to knit works that could be constructed in parts and carried so she could take advantage of every opportunity to add a few stitches.

Lindsay's familiarity with the looping processes of knit and crochet is lifelong. She cannot recall seeing her maternal grandmother without either knitting needles or a cooking spoon in her hand. She learned to crochet from the women on the paternal side of her family. The idea that the time invested in knitting often symbolizes love in American culture is an element that Lindsay plays with in her knitted artworks. "There is also an element of mindfulness in knitting," she says. "It requires attention—if you drop a stitch, it unravels."

When Lindsay works with knitting in performance, she enjoys a direct interaction with her audience. "It's more intimate than the formal encounters with audiences at gallery openings or artist talks," she explains. "My performance work often speaks to the connections between self and other, highlighting and nurturing these fragile tendrils."

Connection performance in downtown Chicago | Lindsay Obermeyer and daughter Emily | 1998
Lindsay and her daughter Emily wore hand-knit mohair sweaters connected by fifteen-foot-long sleeves and interacted with people they met along the way. *Photograph by Audrey Mandelbaum*

Lindsay's *Red Thread Project* acknowledges in a physical way the fact that we are all connected. Large numbers of people become involved at each performance venue. To prepare for the event, as many hats as possible are knit by local volunteers. Lindsay connects each hat to a red knitted I-cord a quarter-mile in length. Onsite, volunteer performers don the hats and move around to Lindsay's choreography. The process makes them very aware of being connected to each other; not moving in synch with your neighbor will result in losing your hat—literally—and being eliminated from the game. Afterward, the hats are disconnected and donated to local cancer patients, foster children, the homeless, or anyone else in need in the community. So far, more than 2,000 hats have been created through the project.

As Lindsay explains, "The *Red Thread Project* is a way to feel connected to the many people who affect my life but whom I don't know. There is the fellow mining the metal to be used in the fork I would one day purchase and daily use, the teachers who taught my teachers, the police officers patrolling my neighborhood—so many people. There is my daughter and the fact that she is adopted. We've developed a bond, a connection that is as strong as that of blood relations, yet I respect and cherish her feeling of connection to her birth parents. There is the charity component to the project, with hats being donated to cancer patients. I am a cancer survivor and know that fear and the need for comfort and connection past the confines of the hospital."

Red Thread performances have been held so far in Indianapolis, Indiana, Memphis, Tennessee, Grand Rapids, Michigan, and a 2008 performance will be held in St. Louis, Missouri. Lindsay has set up a website for the project and plans to write a book on the

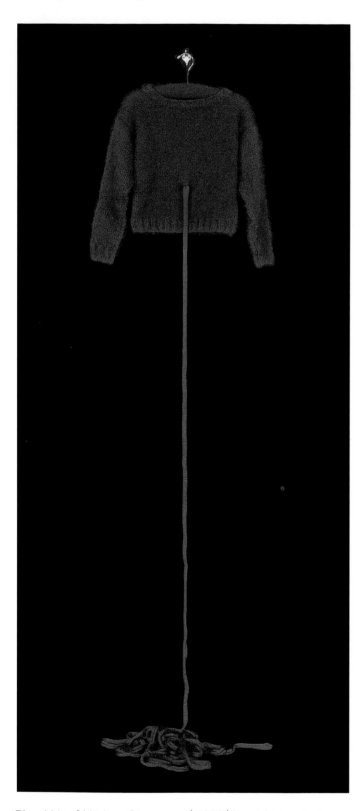

Blood Line | Lindsay Obermeyer | 2006 | hand-knit mohair with machine-knit rayon cord | 19" x 19" w/15" cord
This piece from Lindsay's *Woman's Work* series considers the mother-child bond, which can stretch, rip, fray, or unravel as the child grows and matures. *Photograph by Larry Sanders*

concept with pictures of performances, letters from participants, and a collection of her hat patterns.

Lindsay participated in two of artist Anni Holm's Chicago performance projects involving knitting. In *Networking Project*, knitters constructed a huge web on stage. Holm also organized a group of four knitter-performers to become the world's first knitting band—with bells on their needles and hats—knitting outdoors in wintertime with gloves on.

Lindsay's first foray into public sculpture occurred during the summer of 2007 when she won a commission to knit a giant blue globe for Chicago's Cool Globes: Hot Ideas for a Cooler Planet, a public art project to inspire action against global warming. More than 120 globes, each five feet in diameter, were displayed along Chicago's downtown lakefront between June and October 2007. Lindsay's globe, which she nicknamed "Big Blue," is titled *Adjust the Thermostat* and was the only textile globe included in the project. She knit it in polyester braid with green and gold land and blue water, and it was installed in Grant Park at the entrance to the Field Museum. To "knit a sweater for the world" Lindsay enlisted the help of a high school geometry teacher and his students to work out the complex mathematical progressions of increases and decreases she would need to follow in order to cover the huge sphere. The trials and travails of Lindsay's globe-knitting process are documented on her weblog Serendipity on her website, www.lbostudio.com. She says of this adventure, "It took three weeks, approximately thirty pounds of polyester hollow braid, seven #17, forty seven-inch Addi Turbo circular needles, countless blisters, an addiction to glucosamine, and nightly soaks with Epsom salts."

When she is not creating beaded embroideries in the basement studio of her Chicago home or knitting on the bus or in performance venues, Lindsay exhibits her work widely, gardens, writes articles, designs knit and crochet patterns for publishers such as Lark Books and Interweave Press, and occasionally curates exhibitions. She also teaches adult knitting classes and children's art classes, which she especially enjoys, because, she says, "I can let my silly out." She also enjoys writing her weblog, where she reflects on art, gardening, and life in general.

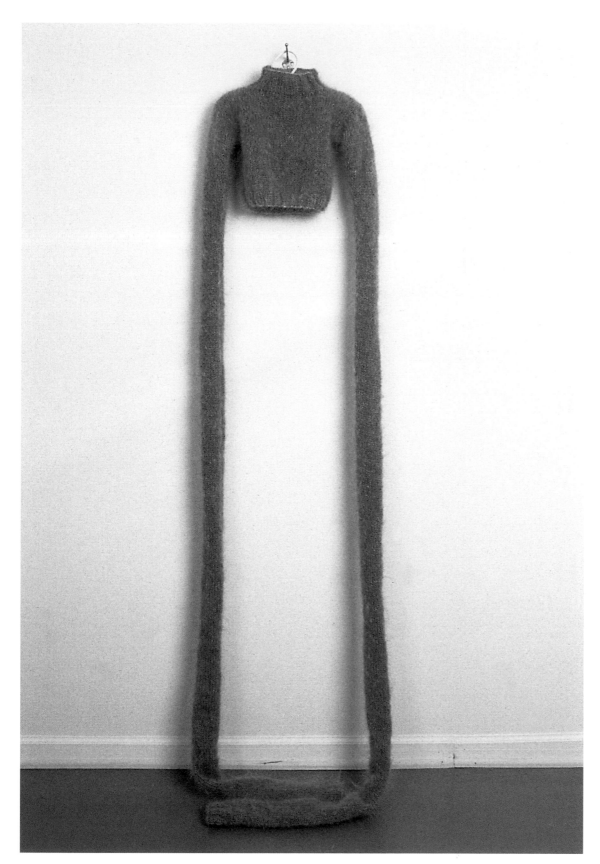

Mommy | Lindsay Obermeyer | 2001 | hand-knit mohair | 11" x 11" body with 84" sleeves
Using a child's sweater form, *Mommy* speaks to the longing for comfort and the panic caused when it is lost.

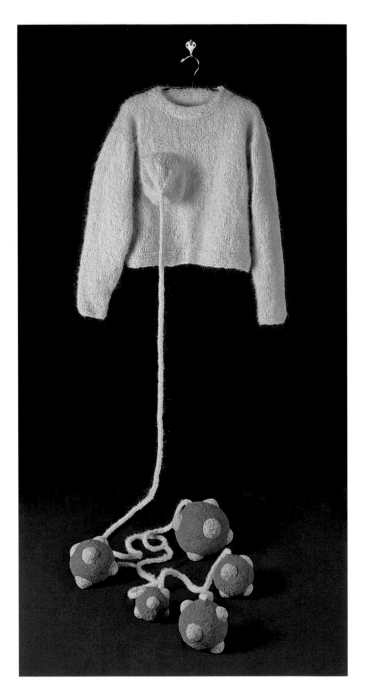

Knocked Out | Lindsay Obermeyer | 2006 | hand-knit mohair with plastic balls | 20" x 20" with 54" cords
This sweater sculpture is part of Lindsay's *Woman's Work* series, which examines the responsibilities and burdens of motherhood.
Photograph by Larry Sanders

Genetic Inheritance | Lindsay Obermeyer | 2006 | hand-knit mohair and felted wool | 20" x 22" w/ five balls
This piece in Lindsay's *Woman's Work* series considers traits passed from mother to child, including tendencies for illnesses, such as cancer. *Photograph by Larry Sanders*

Adjust the Thermostat | Lindsay Obermeyer | 2007 | outdoor sculpture, hand-knit polyester twine covering an acrylic globe | 5' x 5'
Lindsay's "Big Blue" globe sculpture was installed in Chicago's Grant Park in 2007 during the public art event, Cool Globes: Hot Ideas for a Cooler
Planet. Each of the 120 artists' globes in the installation offered a suggestion to help prevent global warming. *Photograph by Lisa Fedich*

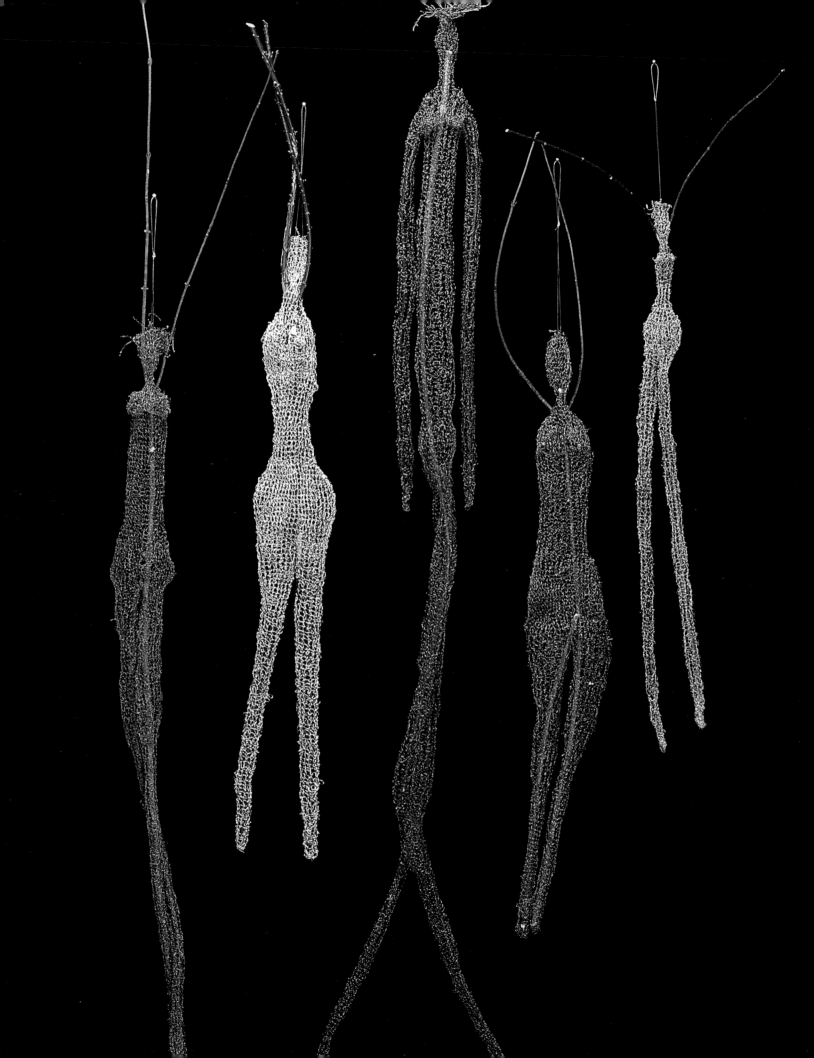

Carolyn Halliday

Carolyn Halliday knits in her studio with her cat, Bonkers. *Photograph by Barbara Gutkin*

Carolyn Halliday's hand-knit sculptures and garment forms make wry comments on women's love/hate relationships with their bodies. The cultural history of clothing fascinates her, as does the fun and playfulness of fashion. Her alternative knitwear collections created for the Textile Center of Minnesota's juried Artwear in Motion fashion event have featured wearable garments in wire and natural materials such as birch bark. One collection was based on string skirts, the earliest-known womens' garments, thought to be symbols of fertility. The song, "Girls Just Want To Have Fun," plus her niece's obsession with the TV show *Sex and the City,* provided the basis for her 2006 collection. "So many people love that show because of its emphasis on fashion. I'm making fun of the tyranny of fashion and also acknowledging that I succumb to it myself," she admits. Her unconventional wardrobe made from industrial materials supplied by a local recycling center includes a hot-pink jacket with aluminum stampings, a group of wire-and-paper cocktail dresses, and a mini-skirt and tie in plastic-coated wire lined with duct tape.

Carolyn stretches the definition of textile by using nontraditional materials in her knitted sculptures, nests, garments, and quilt forms. "I want to believe that the rhythmic repetition of my stitches imbues my forms with an essential energy that can't be replicated by machine," she says of her work. The use of handmade paper is a distinguishing feature of her sculptures. Dipping knitted wire mesh into paper pulp transforms the knitted surface into a rough canvas. Once the paper dries, she can paint it with a rich layering of color, obtaining a crinkled cloth-like texture suggestive of ancient textile fragments.

Carolyn learned knitting as a child from her mother and enjoyed knitting her own fashion sweaters. As a young adult, she learned handspinning and thereafter spun all of her knitting yarns. She began to explore knitting as an artform after attending a workshop taught by Mary Walker Phillips. Through her interest in knitting, Carolyn also became interested in the history that is transmitted through

Stick Figures | Carolyn Halliday | 2003 | hand-knit copper wire and twigs, varying sizes to 56" Twigs provide a natural element as well as a gesture in Carolyn's *Stick Figures* series. The elongated, slender, wire-clad, female forms comment on our cultural preference for thinness. *Photograph by Petronella Ytsma*

Love Song to Andros, detail | 2006 | Carolyn Halliday | hand-knit copper wire, found shells | 5' tall
Carolyn's unique knitted "quilts" pay tribute to domestic textiles and to the wonders of nature. She created pockets in double-knitting and filled them with shells she gathered on a Caribbean beach. Additional shells are stitched onto the surface. *Photograph by Petronella Ytsma*

handmade domestic textiles, or women's work. As she became more aware of the historical importance of knitting, her artwork became more symbolic of the feminine legacy in culture and in textiles. "It feels like a way to claim, or rewrite, women's history," she says, "and also to hold on to the importance of the handmade. It would be a great loss to our culture if we didn't keep the textile traditions alive."

Carolyn's earliest knitted sculptures were folk-style toys in her own handspun wool. She had become intrigued with the technique of *double knitting* and found it a pleasing way to form animals and figures. Her then-young son challenged her to think about shaping when he asked her to create different animals. Soon she began an ongoing series of female figures and torsos, incorporating the psychological insights into women's body issues gleaned through her training and practice as a therapist. Her sculptures celebrate the natural beauty of the female form, however imperfect, while acknowledging the ambivalent relationship that women

often have with their bodies. In her *Stick Figures* series, elements of gesture drawing appear, along with a subtle message about American culture's preference for thinness to the point of encouraging anorexia.

Further experiments with double-knitting revealed a way for Carolyn to enshrine bits of nature in her work. She could incorporate bark, stones, leaves, or cast paper forms between the layers of her double-walled vessels. She could also create "pockets" to fill with sticks, shells, leaves, or even food items. A series of double-knit "quilts" emerged, to which she could add stitching—through the layers or onto the surface. Works such as her *Tree Salutation* series incorporating twigs, and *Love Song to Andros,* incorporating shells, conform to the parameters of "quilt" as defined by art quilt makers: three layers of any sort, held together by some stitching; thus relating these works to the larger vocabulary of textiles.

Inspirations for Carolyn's art works come from her deep emotional connections to nature and the human

My Father's Religion |
Carolyn Halliday | 2007 |
hand-knit copper wire |
7' tall
Carolyn's installation of
hand-knit copper wire
trees recalls her childhood
in northern Minnesota.
Photograph by Peter Lee

Tree Salutation: Winter | Carolyn Halliday | 2005 | hand-knit copper wire, twigs, glass beads
In this knitted wire "quilt," twigs gathered in wintertime are incorporated into double-knit pockets. This piece is part of Carolyn's *Tree Salutation* series of four knitted "quilts" celebrating the four seasons. *Photograph by Petronella Ytsma*

experience. "Something happens physiologically and psychologically when we make stuff," she says. She knits with the multiple strands of seeing, knowing, and responding to materials. In her garment forms, knowledge of textile history and observations about our cultural attachment to highlighting female sexuality become entwined with her own passions for fashion, food, and the outdoors. The themes of containing and releasing informed her early figurative sculptures. Now she is paying more attention to events in her life and her personal obsessions. "I try to notice what's going on around me. Our emotional worlds are fascinating: our everyday experiences have an impact on how we choose to move in a particular direction," she says. She began a series of wire-and-paper nests when her son went off to college, only later realizing that they mirrored her own empty-nest state. The series *Love and Addiction*, a tribute to her favorite things—

coffee, chocolate, and the beauty of nature—includes a huge espresso pot in wire and birch bark, a "quilt" called *How to Eat a Hersheyet* that is filled with candy, and a second "quilt" filled with coffee beans.

Another body of work dealing with memory and memorialization includes assemblages of fabrics with silkscreen-printed images of knitted wire along with vintage items. These works examine memory through the traces of what is left behind; they also explore questions of what makes a textile a textile. *Memorial to my Lost Brother* consists of a reconstructed birch tree trunk, the bark segments reconnected with knitted wire. The stitches provide a rich metaphor for life's structure. It will become part of an installation of wire tree forms called *My Father's Religion*. Carolyn posts a gallery of her work on www.myartspace.com.

Materials in themselves are also a source of artistic inspiration. "I'm repeatedly entranced by the

Perfect Nest | Carolyn Halliday | 2006 | hand-knit copper wire, paper pulp, acrylic paint, glass beads | 3" h x 5" w x 3" d
Carolyn often dips her knitted wire works into paper pulp, which gives her a new surface on which to paint and embellish with beads or stitching. This piece is the size of a small bird's nest. *Photograph by Petronella Ytsma*

exquisite beauty of a piece of bark, a rock, or a stick, and such materials often become the starting point," Carolyn remarks. "Manmade materials are intriguing, too. The most mundane material is beautiful and interesting when constructed."

Carolyn has a cozy studio filled with yarn and spools of wire in the Minneapolis home where she lives with her husband and son. She can often be found knitting while curled up in an easy chair with a purring cat nestled in her lap. She works intuitively with wire and other unusual materials in simple stitches, keeping the emphasis on the emerging form. It's not in her nature to do in-depth planning, and Carolyn marvels at anyone who can make detailed drawings beforehand. She follows her stitches, enjoying the discoveries she makes as a piece progresses, working from an image in her mind

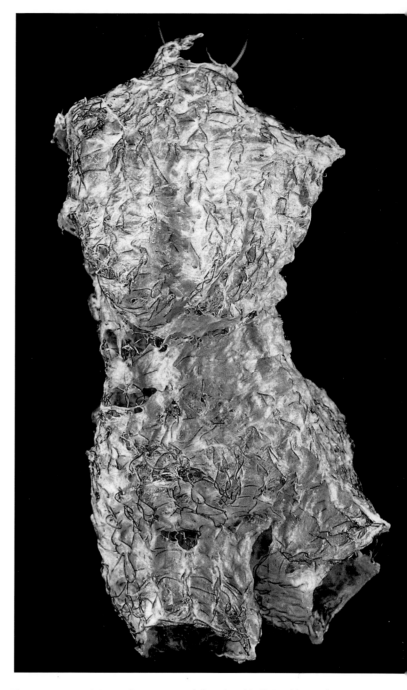

Deconstructed Body Quilt: Torso | Carolyn Halliday | 2004 | hand-knit copper wire, paper pulp | 9" x 12"
This wire and paper sculpture is one panel of a knit and paper "quilt" that celebrates the beauty of imperfect female bodies. *Photograph by Petronella Ytsma*

and thinking about the shape and what is needed technically to achieve it: increases, decreases, or short rows. "I like that knitting is a puzzle, and how you can shape with it. It means something to me that a piece is knit. Textiles matter. The process matters—it's as simple as that."

Tuxedo Dress | Carolyn Halliday | 2004 | hand-knit copper wire, paper pulp, acrylic paint

Carolyn created *Tuxedo Dress*, a wearable wire garment, for a runway fashion show. She dipped a knitted copper wire dress into paper pulp, which gave it a rough, fabric-like texture. She added color with acrylic paint. *Photograph by Petronella Ytsma*

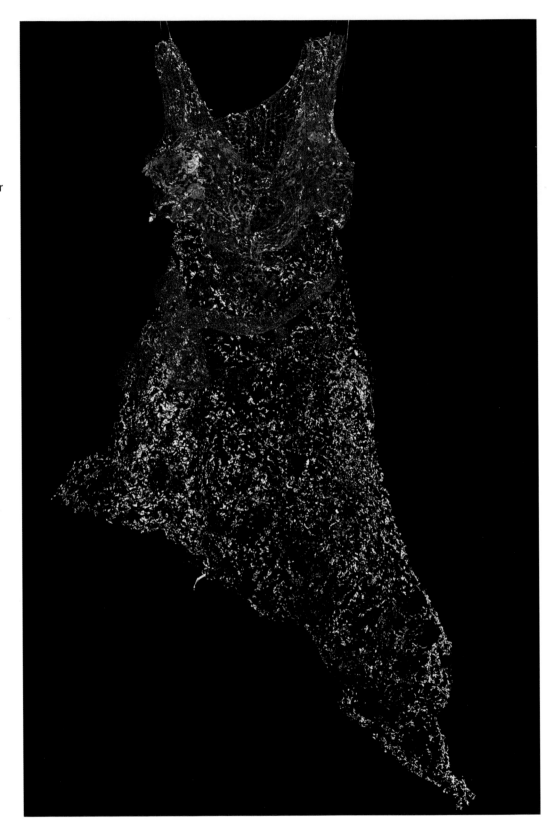

Yeah, Baby I'm a Goddess |
Carolyn Halliday | 2006 |
hand-knit copper wire,
paper pulp, acrylic paint,
polyester
Carolyn created this elegant
copper cocktail dress for a
runway fashion show.

Reina Mia Brill

Reina Mia Brill

Each one of Reina Mia Brill's fey knitted creatures has a story to tell. Their exotic names suggest ideas or visions steeped in mythology. Knitting lends an appealing texture to the light-reflective wire that is her favorite material. Their tactile surfaces invite touch. When the sparkling figures are first seen from a distance, they appear to be beaded. At closer range, it becomes clear that they're made of wire and that they're knitted. "I like the mystery of them—and I like fooling people," Reina says. Like Liza Lou, an artist who wants to cover the world with beads, Reina wants to cover the world with wire.

The figures flow naturally from Reina's imagination and from a belief that creatures are in her blood. "I used to play creature-drawing games with my father," she recalls. "He would draw a creature, and I would draw another one in some active relation to it, and we would continue taking turns, adding to this emerging creature story until the page was full." Her imagery also comes from childhood experiences and memories, a love of children's books, and a fascination with animation. Watching children is another source of inspiration for Reina, as she masterfully captures their mischievous expressions. "Children's thought processes are transparent—you can see when they are being devious," she comments.

A native New Yorker, Reina received her BA in accessory design from the Fashion Institute of Technology in Manhattan. She designed hats, bags, and shoes before switching coasts to work on her MFA degree in jewelry design at San Diego State University.

Reina had wanted to knit with wire for a long time and was finally able to work in this medium near the end of her academic career, when she enrolled in a metals class taught by Arline Fisch. But she needed to learn the basics of knitting first,

Surprise | Reina Mia Brill | 2006 | machine-knit copper wire and silver-plated wire, nylon, resin, wood | 42" x 21" x 10"

Reina created a mini-installation of her figures *Capheira* and *Modibo* for the 2007 International Fiber Art Triennial Exhibition in Lödz, Poland. The figures' outer shells are constructed from layers of knit wire, meticulously stitched over fabric forms with wooden armatures. She constructed a wooden platform so the pair may be viewed at eye level. *Photograph by D. James Dee*

Triloka | Reina Mia Brill | 2007 | machine-knit nontarnish silver-plated wire, nylon, resin, wood | 27" x 12" x 11" *Triloka's mischievous expression and gesture belie the stability of her conical body. Photograph by Steve Gyurina*

If You Keep Making Faces | Reina Mia Brill | 2005 | machine-knit coated copper wire, resin, paint | mama is 10" x 6.5" x 9", child figure is 7" x 4" x 3"
Reina's small mama and child sculptures are constructed with meticulous detail and capture a typical parent–child interaction. *Photograph by D. James Dee*

so she turned to her grandmother for some lessons. Focused on her goal, she practiced her knit and purl stitches with wire. Her new knitting skill came in handy during a six-month stint as a visiting student in the Constructed Textile Department at Duncan of Jordanstone College of Art at Scotland's Dundee University. There she shaped three-dimensional knitted forms on two needles, forming cones and other elements that she assembled into playful, distinctive jewelry items.

On returning to San Diego State, Reina continued to use the shaped wire forms in her jewelry, and she also learned to use wire on knitting machines. She received her MFA in 1997 and returned to New York to set up a design studio in Manhattan, making and selling her colorful jewelry. In 2001, she began working on a series of figurative sculptures. At first, she worked the 28-gauge wire for her figures by hand on size-one

needles, but she quickly found it hard on her hands and turned to her knitting machine. She knits the wire fabric that covers her sculptures on a 1960s-vintage double-bed machine. She also uses an antique sock-knitting machine (ca. 1923) that she found on e-Bay to knit the softer fabrics she uses as the base layer for the faces of her mythical figures.

The creatures' personalities evolve through a complex process. First, Reina constructs a wooden "skeleton" for support and for posture. Then she wraps fabric or foil and cotton batting over the form, building its shape. Nylon fabric serves as the top layer of a padded "skin" that covers the armatures. Several layers of stockinette-stitch wire fabric in different colors are then painstakingly stitched down over this skin to create subtle color-shading effects. In the process of hand stitching the wire layers, she also forms and shapes the features. In describing her

Cheruba | Reina Mia Brill | 2004 | machine-knit nontarnish silver-plated wire, resin, and paint | 8.5" x 8" x 6"
This vessel/figure appears ready to take flight. *Photograph by D. James Dee*

Divalia | Reina Mia Brill | 2006 | machine-knit coated
copper wire, nylon, resin, wood | 29" x 15" x 11"
Divalia's coy expression may be due to the fact that she is traveling in
the 2007 Fiber Art International, which opened at the Pittsburgh Center
for the Arts and tours the United States through 2009. *Photograph by D.
James Dee*

process, Reina says, "Panels of knitted wire are layered,
like pen and ink drawings, to create surface tension and
drama. Each wire stitch is meticulously placed into the
wire fabric—layer by layer, over faces, horns, and even
the crevices of toes—until the essence of each creature
breathes life. I start with the face. That dictates how
the rest of the figure will look." In the figures' clothing,
she uses pattern stitches to add another element of
dimension and interest to the garments.

In 2005, Reina relocated her home and studio
from Manhattan to a remote section of the Bronx
called City Island, where, she says, "the nature-filled
surroundings are inspiring a new generation of
creatures." Many are pictured on her website,
www.reinamiabrill.com, and she records some of
her art adventures in a weblog. She made a bold
decision to devote herself full-time to her art and
has immersed herself in exploring new directions in
her work. Groups of figures posed in relation to each
other are emerging in small installations. She is also
designing environments or settings for her figures
and making some larger sculptures. She has begun to
work with clay and is excited about the possibilities of
combining it with knitted wire.

Reina's knitted jewelry appears in several books
on contemporary art jewelry and in *Artwear: Fashion
and Anti-Fashion* by Melissa Leventon. Her sculptures
appear in *Fiberarts Design Book 7* and *Textile
Techniques in Metal* (2001 edition) by Arline Fisch,
and most recently, *500 Handmade Dolls* (2006). She
shows her work in numerous exhibitions and galleries
in the United States and internationally, and she has
received numerous awards for her work. She enjoys
making the rounds of the fine-craft show circuit,
where she can meet the people who collect her work.
Surprise, a figure duo, and her largest work so far,
was accepted into the prestigious 12th International
Triennial of Tapestry held in Lödz, Poland, in 2007,
and she traveled to Poland to attend the opening. She
was one of six American artists selected to participate
in the exhibition and the only "emerging artist" among
the American exhibitors.

Avaric | Reina Mia Brill | 2006 | machine-knit coated copper wire, resin, paint | 12" x 4" x 5" Reina has captured a childlike expression of contentment in *Avaric*'s stitched wire expression. *Photograph by D. James Dee*

Elowedd | Reina Mia Brill | 2004 | machine-knit nontarnish silver-plated wire, resin, and brass | 12" x 11" x 6"
This wire wall figure is posed in mid-action, holding up a flower to be admired. *Photograph by D. James Dee*

Adrienne Sloane

Adrienne Sloane

Knitting for Adrienne Sloane is a metaphor about connection: knitting together the frayed edges of our lives. She appreciates knitting's flexibility, its geometry, and its dimensionality as she creates her thoughtful art works. For eighteen years, Adrienne designed, produced, and sold distinctive, colorful, sculptural hats on the fine-craft fair circuit. Hats were most appealing to her, since she could use them as quick studies for exploring form and color combinations. She could let her imagination run wild, yet still produce functional, saleable items. Now she is exploring material and form in exciting new ways.

"If I had gone to art school, I would have done sculpture," Adrienne muses. Two streams of work are emerging from her current explorations in hand and machine knitting. She is intrigued with the sculptural possibilities of *knitting-on*, a yarn-painting or knitted appliqué technique that she had explored in her hats and now applies to container forms and whimsical sculptures. A more serious body of work focuses on war and other political issues, de-emphasizing color and using monochromatic materials such as wire and natural linen in poignant multiple images. "While I enjoy the clever or whimsical and color work very much, I find that I want to use my craft to make an emotional impact about important issues," she says. Her installations *Truth to Power* and *Cost of War* "are anti-war expressions that are immediate responses to the current political climate but also are timeless responses to the brutality of war."

Born in Manhattan and raised in Westchester County, New York, Adrienne comes from a family of artists: her grandmother, father, and sister are all painters. Adrienne and her sister were encouraged to attend arts classes throughout their childhood. Her mother taught her to knit. "I can remember waiting for her to return home from work to pick up my dropped stitches at around age ten," she recalls.

Ode to a Leaky Urn | Adrienne Sloane | 2006 | machine-knit cotton | 9" h x 10.5" w x 7.5" d
Adrienne's humorous vessel is decorated with sculptural appliquéd elements. First she knits a solid-color base, then attaches colored strips to its purl side using a process she calls "yarn painting," or "knitting-on."
Photograph by Joe Ofria

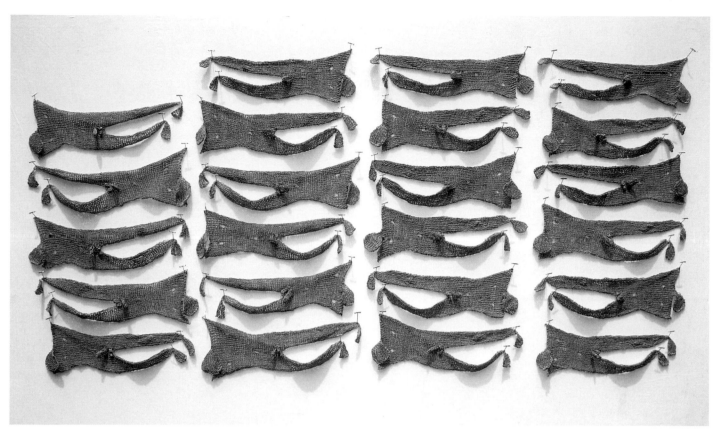

Cost of War | Adrienne Sloane | 2006 | machine-knit linen rug warp | 30" h x 62" w
Adrienne's moving wall installation consists of twenty-four linen male bodies. From a distance, they appear to form an abstract design, but close up they tell another story. *Photograph by Joe Ofria*

Opposite page:
Truth to Power installation | Adrienne Sloane | 2007 | machine-knit wire | 62" (ceiling) h x 24" w x 36" d
In Adrienne's dramatic room-sized lament on war, wire bodies freefall in space toward pools of blood-red wire on the ground. Adrienne's inspiration came from listening to daily news broadcasts on the war situation while working in her studio. *Photograph by Joe Ofria*

Adrienne's educational background is in anthropology, and she has traveled extensively in Europe and Central Asia. She spent a year in India and another year and a half in Southeast Asia, mainly Malaysia and Indonesia. "I traveled for three years (on the cheap) during the early 1970s, which I have often considered to be my graduate degree," she says. Returning to the United States in 1974, Adrienne moved to California, where she learned to spin and weave, and then to Vermont to earn a master's degree in teaching English as a Second Language.

On moving to the Boston area in 1981 to work on the World Affairs Council of Boston's program for foreign students, Adrienne purchased a used knitting machine on a whim and learned to use it. Knitting's tactile, textural qualities enticed her. She built up her hat business, which flourished through 1998, adapting it to her increasingly busy family life after her son

was born. Of this productive period, she says, "I made a pact with myself never to rip out anything I didn't like, or I would never finish a piece. If I didn't like an unusual color combination, someone else would."

After a horrific studio building fire in 1999 in which many artists lost all of their work and equipment, Adrienne closed her studio and business and became involved in local arts administration and arts advocacy activities. She was instrumental in starting an art center in her hometown of Watertown, Massachusetts (The Arsenal Center for the Arts), and she still serves on its board of directors. She also began teaching classes locally in handknitting and freeform knitting.

Adrienne had been able to salvage her knitting machines and some yarns from the fire, and after a while the yarns began calling to her. She used some of them to make hooked pictures and liked the painterly and textural effects she could achieve in rug hooking.

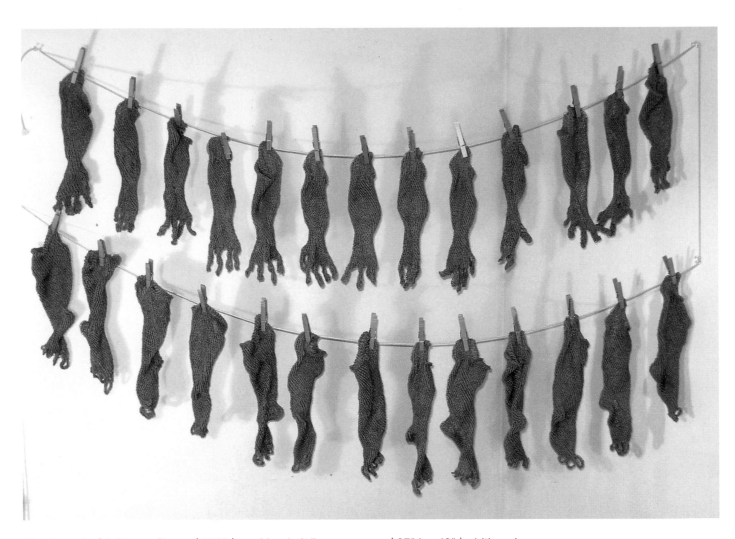

Dirty Laundry | Adrienne Sloane | 2006 | machine-knit linen rug warp | 37" h x 40" | width varies
In this confrontational work expressing anti-war sentiments, Adrienne displays multiple knitted hands and feet on a clothesline.

Soon, her dining room was full of fiber, and she realized that it was time to look for another studio. She found space on the third floor of a former elementary school reincarnated as an arts center in nearby Lexington. Wondering if she still remembered how to use her knitting machines several years after the fire, she set one up and tried it out. "And the possibilities were again immediately compelling," she says. "I started with some small pieces in the rescued cottons, intrigued that I picked up with concepts pretty much where I had left off. I had no idea where it would lead and little idea of who was doing sculptural knitting or how it was happening out in the world." She enrolled in two summer workshops—one taught by Donna Lish and the other with Katharine Cobey—and has produced an impressive body of work since then.

"I tend to do a lot of shaping and short rowing, taking advantage of the strengths of machine knitting,"

Adrienne says. "I also handknit, which opens other doors." She works on sculpture studies using wire and linen on her machine, or doing handknitting and finger knitting with bed sheets and other large-scale materials. Such monochromatic works have freed her to focus on the form itself, drawing on the same sculptural geometry that is used to shape clothing. She has three punch-card knitting machines: two are standard-bed machines and one is for bulky yarns.

In an effort to combine her love of fiber with her dedication to helping those in the developing world, Adrienne seeks volunteer opportunities with textile artisan cooperatives abroad. She worked with knitting projects in Bolivia in the falls of 2002 and 2006, and in Peru in the summers of 2005 and 2006. She currently serves on the board of directors for Weave a Real Peace (WARP), which assists textile cooperatives in developing countries worldwide.

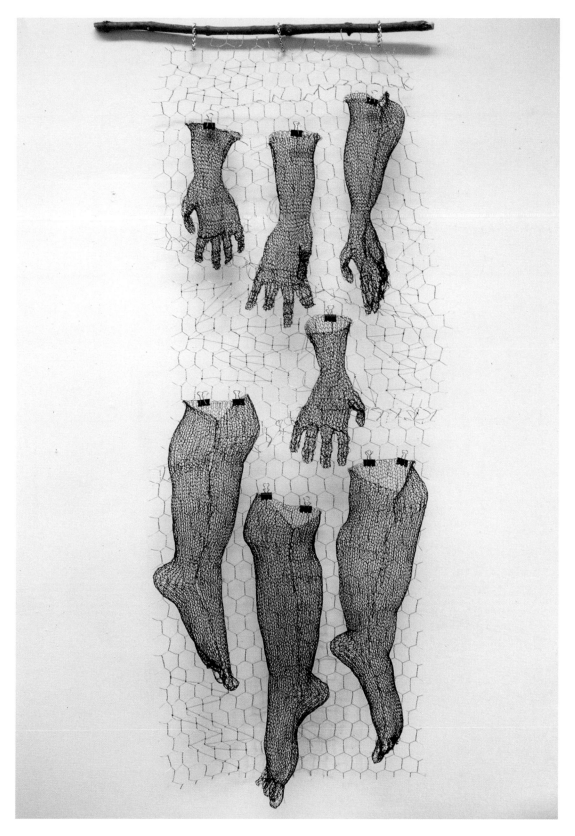

Body Count | Adrienne Sloane | 2007 | machine-knit wire, chicken wire, metal clips, branch | 18" w x 52" h x 6" d

Adrienne knit and shaped the arms and legs for this composition as flat pieces on the knitting machine. Her red seam stitches add both dimension and drama to the piece.

Pencil Box | Adrienne Sloane | 2004 | machine-knit cotton | 7" h x 8" w x 8" d

Adrienne decorated her knit *Pencil Box* using the yarn-painting process, then threaded the pencils through the loops of its knitted embellishments.

Photograph by Munya Avigail Upin

Tea for Two | Adrienne Sloane | 2006 | machine-knit cotton
Adrienne shaped these teapots on the knitting machine, then embellished their surfaces with layers of color and texture in yarn painting. She knits each color strip on the machine, and as it grows she attaches it at intervals to the teapot.

Lisa Anne Auerbach

Lisa Anne Auerbach
models her *Take Back
Red Sash*.

Lisa Anne Auerbach's sweaters sporting edgy and ironic statements challenge many of knitting's nostalgic and domestic stereotypes. Her knitting is an art-making strategy for drawing attention to war and other pressing social issues. Lisa's *Body Count Mittens*, for example, monitor United States and Iraqi war casualties, and her sweaters quote political speak or ask questions such as, "What's your favorite thing about the war on terror?" on the front, with the wearer's answer on the back. Knitted banners and manifestos offer a visual invitation to think about and discuss a particular message. America's long history of women knitting for the troops in wartime influenced Lisa's decision to knit such works. She urges knitters to "stop making scarves, start making trouble!"

Her recent body of knitted work was inspired by the sweaters worn by singer Rick Nielsen of the pop music group Cheap Trick. "They were weird, custom, and frequently adorned with random snippets of text, like 'Don't Steal My Girlfriend,' or the band's name placed upside down so only he could read it. I was struck by the friction between the permanence of the material and the liveliness of the language and content," Lisa says. She decided to use the sweater as a canvas for making topical statements, contrasting the durability of the sweater with the immediacy of its message.

By 2004, she was able to invest in a computerized knitting machine, which became an essential tool for making topical work, as it allows her to knit a response to something within a few days. She may write her own texts, or the words may come from current events reporting, popular songs, or other writings. Lisa uses language skillfully, injecting humor and subtle irony to turn political doublespeak on its ear. At the same time, she maintains what she calls a "pro-positive" outlook:

Body Count Mittens | Lisa Anne Auerbach | 2005 | hand-knit merino wool mittens
The body count number for the war in Iraq changed during the week that passed between finishing the first mitten and starting the second, so Lisa revised the number in the second mitten. This first pair of *Body Count Mittens* was knit in 2005 and is part of a group of works in which she tracks United States and Iraqi war casualties.

Body Count Sweater, Aug. 9, 2005 | Lisa Anne Auerbach | 2005 | machine-knit merino wool sweater
Lisa set out to make a sweater that would embody history the moment it was made. By the day she made this sweater, 1,838 American soldiers had been killed in Iraq. The back says, "Freedom frightens the enemy. And it's messy"; two assertions made by United States government officials. Motifs of guns and coffins accompany a traditional yoke design.

"Being in favor of that which is both beneficial and progressive. If you put bad vibes into a garment, it becomes itchy and uncomfortable," she says.

Her first efforts on the knitting machine were sweaters bearing slogans in support of her favorite presidential candidate. Then she turned to themes in the news: abortion, the war in Iraq, Hurricane Katrina, and other timely issues. She quoted 1960s Weather Underground slogans, juxtaposing them with meteorological imagery on three sweaters made for an exhibition at the Kunstahl in Copenhagen in 2006, inspired by a Danish TV weather broadcaster who always wore hand-knit sweaters on the air.

Lisa makes her sweaters appear somewhat traditional. "Part of the definition of a sweater for me is the heritage of traditional designs like Fair Isle and Norwegian motifs," she says. She uses a merino wool yarn for a sturdy fabric, sticking to classic sweater shapes for timeless styles, and enjoys the fact that her messages are not likely to stay in synch with the styles. For instance, the *Body Count* sweaters and mittens were current only on the day that they were made. "By the following morning, the statistics were history," she says.

Lisa's architectural works include banners that cover a wall and long, narrow ones that can encircle

To Say "I Love You" Means Let the Revolution Begin | Lisa Anne Auerbach | 2005 | machine-knit merino wool banner
This limited edition banner was inspired by a paragraph written on social justice and love by Carter Heyward. Lisa created a panel
that can be worn as a garment or flaunted as a proclamation.

a room. In an all-text piece, the words form patterns of their own making, and she is fascinated to notice which words stand out and which ones recede. Her largest text work to date is *Take Back Red*, an eleven-foot-wide American flag knit in red and pink, containing her impassioned, knitted-in manifesto written in the style of the Italian Futurist artists of the 1950s. It is a love poem to the color red and laments its cooptation for political purposes, claiming that the United States is too complex a nation to be divided into merely red and blue states. "Red is ours, and we want it back," it begins. "Red, the color of passion, anger, love, and whores, was stolen out from under our feet, replaced with the serenity of ninny blue . . . ."

To prepare for knitting, Lisa digitizes an image in Photoshop and downloads it into the machine 200 rows at a time. "I had an idea that a machine meant you push a button and a sweater pops out, but it's really pretty high-tech," she says. She handknits smaller projects, such as mittens and hats. A separate studio building is located in the back yard of the hundred-year-old Los Angeles bungalow that she and her husband are renovating. Its two rooms are filled with yarn, her knitting machine and computers, her sewing machine, and various handknitting projects.

Raised in a Chicago suburb, Lisa learned sewing as a child from her quiltmaker mother. She studied photography and received a BFA from Rochester Institute of Technology in 1990 and her MFA from Art Center College of Design in Pasadena, California, in 1994. She turned to knitting after graduation, during a time when she was without a darkroom, teaching herself by following the instructions in a library book. Her first project was a Lopi ski sweater. Her hand-knit sweaters were simpler in design than the machine-knit missives, with more personal imagery, and, of course, her production rate was much slower.

Lisa is an adjunct instructor at University of Southern California's Roski School of Fine Arts, where she teaches photography, and she also teaches knitting workshops in the Los Angeles area. She photographs her own work and also works on several ongoing photo-documentation projects. An avid bicyclist and advocate of bike commuting in Los Angeles, Lisa has inspired many Los Angelinos to become bike riders. She documents her riding adventures in a self-published 'zine called *Saddlesore* and in a weblog on her website www.lisaanneauerbach.com. She has also done some performance-based art works with bicycle themes.

Lisa's knitted messages are one aspect of her writing and publishing interests. In addition to writing, illustrating, and publishing several 'zines and writing her biking blog, Lisa keeps a knitting blog on her website www.stealthissweater.com, where she encourages "knitting as an antidote to a culture of fear." Instructions for her *Body Count Mittens* are available on the site.

Knitting for Lisa is an ongoing art practice that leads her to unexpected places. She wants to encourage people to make things that are more interesting than copying an existing garment design. "Here is a medium where you can do anything you want, and people just want to make it look like something that has already been made. I don't understand that at all," she laments. Her "Manifesto for Knitters," originally published in December 2005 in *KnitKnit 6*, speaks eloquently to this issue.

When There's Nothing Left to Burn, Set Yourself on Fire | Lisa Anne Auerbach | 2005 | machine-knit merino wool

In this sweater, Lisa combines a quote from a popular song by The Stars with an image of a suicide belt, alluding to the glorification of self-destruction in American popular culture versus the reality of actual self-destruction. An image of dynamite sticks is used as a decorative motif at the waistline. The yoke has a traditional Turkish design. The words *mort pour rien*, "dead for nothing," can be found on the back of the sweater. This is a reference to riots in Paris at the time, in which two young men were killed by police for trespassing.

This is a call for a dynamic, new direction for knitting!
This is a call for a dynamic, new direction for knitting!

Lay down that eyelash yarn and giant needles, and pick up a project that's thoughtful, elegant, and odd. Let each sweater be something completely new. Forego patterns in favor of making it up yourself.

Go beyond.

Go above.

Figure it out for yourself.

Do not be shy. The time is now; there will never be a better one. Use technology if you have to. Computers are your friends. Knitting machines are ungainly but useful. Reclaim knitting! It is a noble craft; it is NOT the new yoga. Repetitive and unthinking motions will kill the soul. Knitting is creating. Custom sweaters are the new tattoos. Why make the same thing everyone else is making if you don't have to? You have choices: make use of them.

THEN: Knitters who have come before us are remembered for cabled guernseys, paper-thin stockings, mittens and gloves adorned with sonnets or sobriquets, and undergarments fluttering with lace. Our forebears learned to knit at a young age. Small children were started on stockings, knitting in the round. Adolescents turned heels and decreased at the toes.

Look back at the history of knitting, and you will see tiny stitches, fancy flourishes, and complex shaping. Aesthetically speaking, the knitters of yore had it going on. Totally badass, persnickety, and adorable. And, as if incredibly good-looking and fashionable weren't enough for these long-ago knitters, old-time chicks with sticks transformed American culture, no joke. In the 1890s, when a bicycle craze swept the nation, ladies were still wearing duds that might get stuck in the spokes, or worse. Knitting came to the rescue, providing the fashionable a new and sporty choice. Hemlines started to rise, and jaunty knitted stockings became all the rage. It wasn't long before sweaters went from underwear to outerwear, and the rest is history.

Thank our feminist ancestors with yarn and vision for getting us out of the corset and into the sweater. The early part of the twentieth century plugged along just fine, and many a garment was stitched for soldiers, grandchildren, schoolmarms, bachelors, fishermen, and whores. Those who wanted to knit for the war effort used patterns published by the Red Cross for sweaters, vests, gloves, and socks. Fashioning garments was a talent taken for granted. Knitters, it seemed, knew how to knit. And then what happened?

NOW: Like many other things, recent times saw the history of knitting take an unfortunate turn for the worse. Though the popularity of the craft has gone through the roof, we are now faced with an unprecedented epidemic of mediocrity characterized by ultra-bulky yarn and

Take Back Red | Lisa Anne Auerbach | 2006 | machine-knit merino wool banner

Within the giant flag stripes of *Take Back Red*, Lisa has "written" a love poem to her favorite color and her assertion that the United States is too complex a nation to be divided into merely red and blue. It begins, "Red is ours and we want it back." The lettering, knitted in shades of pink and red on the backside of the double-faced fabric, shows through in the lighter stripes.

loosely knit, skinny scarves. Yarn companies are laughing all the way to the bank as they introduce more yarns and patterns that will satisfy knitters with a "scarf in an hour" or a "sweater in a day."

If the current crop of madness does not cease, we in the here and now will be remembered by future knitters as the generation who collapsed the craft. We cannot and must not let this happen! Knitting is not supposed to be easy. Knitting takes time and thought and patience and attention. A well-made sweater will last a lifetime or longer. There's no point in wasting time and money on ugliness.

Down with simple and boring!

Up with thoughtful and complex!

Chart your message, and wear it proudly. Mix yarns and colors. Spice it up. Try the materials of today: Kevlar, retro-reflective, stainless steel, dynamite, yak. Resist fashion. Manufacture your own brand. Embrace tradition. Learn from history. Shatter the present. Create the future. Stitch by stitch, we can and will change the world. The revolution is at hand, and knitting needles are the only weapons you'll need. Stop making scarves; start making trouble.

Consume less.

Create more.

Knitting is political.

BEGIN IMMEDIATELY.

Praise the Lord and Pass the Ammunition | Lisa Anne Auerbach | 2005 | machine-knit merino wool sweater

Lisa made this sweater to commemorate the occasion of ending the ban on assault rifle use in the United States. The dates in which the ban was in effect are knit into the sleeves. She designed the sweater to have a traditional look. Her knitted skirt espouses a "pro-positive, pro-alertness" philosophy.

Quagmire | Lisa Anne Auerbach | 2006 | machine-knit merino wool banner
The word "quagmire," sometimes used in association with the war in Iraq, stands in direct contrast to the prettiness of this banner. The words "shock" and "awe" appear in the borders. Her knitted skirt has bicycle imagery, and her name appears upside down along the bottom border.

Anna Maltz

Anna, wearing her recently completed hand-knit mohair *Gorilla Suit*, made in tribute to the feminist art-activism group, The Guerrilla Girls.

Fuzzy mohair "nude suits" and invisible giant rabbits are humorous, yet edgy works that characterize Anna Maltz's knitted art. This witty artist and social critic received her BFA in 2001 from Middlesex University, London, and is a 2004 MFA graduate of California College of the Arts (CCA), in Oakland, California. She lived in San Francisco before taking up residence in London again in the summer of 2007.

Anna is of Dutch ancestry, born and raised in England. She has considered herself a knitter most of her life. She recalls a picture of herself at age five, sitting on a chair, knitting with her eyes closed, "as my proof of how good I'd gotten." She first viewed knitting as an art medium while spending a semester in Holland in 2000. In the Dutch yarn shops, she saw cards of brightly colored *stopwol,* or darning wool, a material that is obsolete in most places. Intrigued, she bought all the colors and began knitting a scarf. An elderly friend who watched her knit called her Madame Defarge, and Anna decided to read *A Tale of Two Cities* to better understand that reference. "The idea of knitting in a secret code was very inspiring to me," she says. "I decided it was time to make my work like that."

Anna managed to use knitting as her medium in her BFA program, which encouraged students to choose an unfamiliar medium and experiment with it. "We weren't taught the basis of how to do anything—you would go to a technician for that," she explains. "As much as I could understand the reason for that approach, where ignorance turns up all sorts of exciting discoveries, there is a lot to be said for having a skill and knowing enough about how to do it, so you can break away, or push the things you know about it."

While knitting her way to a fine arts degree, Anna started thinking about knowledge and the ways in which people learn. "One way of learning is from the people around you—passing on skills for survival, for life, for satisfaction, or for

Superman Suit | Anna Maltz | 2000 | hand-knit mohair costume | chromogenic print 14" x 9-⅜"
Anna's friend Pien tries on Anna's mohair *Superman Suit.* The scratchy, ill-fitting suit seems to negate the superpowers it boasts.

making people happy. Knitting is a skill that people passed on to me because they cared about me and were interested in me."

Knitting also suited Anna's idea of being an artist in society, as it allows for creating out in the world rather than isolating yourself in a studio. This social aspect of knitting also draws on different areas of knowledge. Anna explains: "People can approach knitting in many ways, such as asking, 'How long did that take you?' When I'm knitting in public, it opens an invitation to people to ask what I'm doing and discuss that with me. Such questions engage their understandings of how things happen."

Anna's first art knitting project was to add impossibly long knitted arms onto found work gloves, while thinking about the care that goes into knitting. "It's almost like a twisted care," she muses, "When something is knitted for you, it's knitted with much love, but the love is also of doing it." Recalling the sweaters her grandmother made for her mother— always with too-long sleeves: "It was because of her idea of my mum's proportions, but also because you get carried away with what you're doing, and who it's for begins to matter less."

An overly large mohair *Superman Suit* ensued. Anna combined the super-masculine hero image with women's work in a big, hairy suit that fits all, but fits

Naked Suits | Anna Maltz | 2001 | hand-knit mohair body suits | chromogenic print 20" x 13-½"
Anna's hand-knit mohair *Naked Suits* are modeled by Melanie, Guy, Emily, and Alice in London. Anna has photographed people from diverse ethnic backgrounds wearing these suits to explore issues of stereotyping and difference.

no one well, and is quite likely to constrict heroic activities. Her suit suggests that everyone can be a hero, while reflecting our human desire for someone to come in and fix everything—a disempowering notion to Anna's mind. She comments: "It's appropriate that this idea of superheroes comes out of American culture and its idea of power."

Anna photographed friends and acquaintances of all ages, sizes, and cultures wearing the suit and exhibits the photos. She likes involving people she knows in her work, and they participate willingly because of the knitting element. "The time invested in knitting is a signifier of its importance but also carries the idea that there is an innocuous quality about it," she says. Photo sessions take place in the models' homes. "I'm being invited into their space, and I'm inviting them into something that I've made. There is trust and sharing within that space. And getting dressed up is fun. The photos are there for others to see part of what happened."

While considering superheroes and unrealistic ideals, Anna saw an ultimate irony in the portrayal of Adam and Eve as a white, heterosexual couple. She set about ordering quantities of pale pink mohair for a pair of anatomically correct male and female body suits. Again, she photographed a diverse array of people wearing the suits. Since she had greatly overestimated her yarn order, she gave the couple three children, and the piece moved on to being a work about difference, illustrated by having the suits worn by people who don't fit the white-nuclear-family model and by those who do.

The many questions Anna was asked about the time element in her knitting provided the impetus for her graduate work at CCA: she sought to make the labor aspect of her work invisible. Intrigued by the use of blue screen in film and video to make things disappear, she searched out its match in yarn.

Anna is an avid film buff and watches movies relating to themes in her work while knitting. In this case, she watched films about invisibility or disappearing. "What struck me is that invisibility is often used to break community and social contracts. If you rape or steal or spy, you break the comfort levels of what you're allowed to do. One of the films I watched was *Harvey*, where an invisible character is used to force the issue of making a family or community decision about mental health. At that point, I decided that my invisible suit would be for

Big Blue Rabbit (visible) | Anna Maltz | 2004 | hand-knit angora costume, window | digital print 20" x 13-½"
Anna's giant bluescreen-blue angora rabbit sits quite visibly in an upper-story window in San Francisco.

Big Blue Rabbit (invisible, nearly) | Anna Maltz | 2004 | hand-knit angora rabbit suit | digital print 5" x 3"
Anna attempted to render her rabbit suit invisible by blending into a bluescreen background, but the angora yarn absorbed just enough light to prevent its total disappearance.

a six-foot, two-and-one-half-inch rabbit. There is something both amusing and empowering about being able to choose to disappear, and to give yourself that power through the unlikely approach of knitting."

Anna's next decision, whether or not to splurge on angora yarn, involved the quintessential artists' conflict between obtaining the perfect material and financial reality. "But, it *had* to be angora—I needed to reconstitute a bunny rabbit!" she exclaimed. She made a video to demonstrate the blue rabbit's disappearance in action, but although its color matched the blue screen perfectly, the rabbit shows up in shadow, due to angora's density and light-absorption qualities.

Anna also creates mixed-media works but really enjoys her knitted ones. She is fascinated by the

renewed interest in knitting in the United States and United Kingdom during the past decade. "Knitting is no longer a necessity; it has become a luxury," she says. "And that divorce from necessity is what makes it an interesting medium to work in. It's also a divorce from a certain kind of history and from the knowledge that everyone shared."

Anna recently finished knitting a black angora gorilla suit for herself, in tribute to the history of the 1970s Feminist Art Movement and the art activism of The Guerrilla Girls. "Part of the dialogue in feminist art is finding alternative ways of making art. Because of work that happened in sixties and seventies I'm able to do the work I do now without having to battle for recognition of my techniques as being valid and accepted as art—for the most part."

Wolf in Sheep's Clothing |
Anna Maltz | 2005 |
silkscreen poster
Anna created this poster for the
exhibition Dumb Economy,
Funny Democracy, Impossible
Projects, curated by Joseph del
Pesco in 2005 at Rooseum in
Malmö, Sweden.

Mermaid Suit | Anna Maltz | 2003 | hand-knit mohair costume | chromogenic print 14" x 9-⅜"
As a child, Anna thought she would like to be a mermaid. Her mohair *Mermaid Suit* has been modeled by several of her friends, including Carl, who was photographed in San Francisco.

Mark Newport

Mark Newport wears *My Batman*, one of his hand-knit superhero costumes.

Mark Newport uses textile processes such as embroidery and knitting to examine traditional male and female roles. His knitted superhero suits embody the hyper-masculine stereotype of the comic book superhero—sort of. Hanging limply on a gallery wall, the knitted suits may invite one viewer to try on this role, but they also suggest the suit's futility, since the knitting would cover the "hero" with a softness that contradicts the macho image. The heroic image is further compromised by the fact that the scratchy suits button up the back, like a pair of old-fashioned children's pajamas.

Mark grew up in New England in the 1960s and 1970s during an era when larger-than-life heroes dominated the print media and the airwaves. His lifelong fascination with heroic comic book figures such as Batman and Superman has inspired him to create art works in knitting, weaving, embroidery, print, photo, performance, and video based on this theme. Through his work, Mark explores ideas of masculinity and brute strength, along with the role of the male as protector. His interest in the drawing techniques of comic book artists also dates back to his boyhood; he taught himself to draw by copying his favorites. Mark attended the Kansas City Art Institute for his BFA degree, received his MFA from the Art Institute of Chicago, and taught in Arizona State University's art department from 1999 to 2006. In 2007, he was appointed Artist-in-Residence at Cranbrook Academy of Art, where he teaches in the graduate program.

Mark's grandmother had taught her rambunctious young grandsons to knit as a quieting-down strategy. Much later, Mark re-learned knitting in order to create his first Batman suit. His wife taught him to cast on and got him going. He learned the basics of shaping garments and plunged into his super heroic knitting adventures. By then, he was the father of two toddlers and was beginning to examine his role in his children's lives, since young children often think their parents are invincible.

Batman 2003 | Mark Newport | hand-knit costume, worsted-weight yarn
Mark's series of suits for comic book characters are proportioned to fit a six-foot-tall male, such as himself. The suits replicate the costumes as illustrated in popular comic books.

An exhibition of Mark's hand-knit superhero suits includes (left to right): *Batman 2, Iron Man, Sweaterman, Every Any No Man, Bobble Man, Aquaman,* and *Rawhide Kid.*

The superhero suits are made in Mark's size and replicate the garb of actual comic book characters. They measure six feet from head to toe, but when hanging in a gallery, they stretch and assume an elongated, specter-like presence. "The viewer begins to imagine the body that would fill it up," he says. "I like to think that someone may want to try them on and take on the role." Knitting seemed the most appropriate technique for executing these works: the stitch-by-stitch construction fits with Mark's process-oriented way of working; its stretchiness fits the imagery; its labor-intensive nature contradicts the implied instantaneous action of the heroes. The humor of Mark's work lies in that juxtaposition.

Mark is particularly fascinated with Batman, because he is human and therefore vulnerable. He has created four distinctly different Batman suits so far in answer to the question, "What does varying the costume do to the hero?" Asking, "What happens when your powers define you?" led him to make the *Fantastic 4* suit for the figure who stretches to become ten feet tall. This overly large garment has a normal-sized neck and sleeves. He is currently exploring the question, "If a superhero had to knit his own costume, how would he act?" The answer lies in the new cast of heroic characters that is emerging from Mark's needles, with pattern stitches serving as the heroes' emblems: *Sweaterman, Bobble Man, Cable Man,* and friends.

Thinking of his new characters and asking, "How would a knitting superhero repel evil by knitting?" Mark recalled his mother and grandmother knitting serenely in the midst of kid-related chaos and concluded that "knitting generates a protective force field around the knitter and around the ones he protects." This group of suits contains some personal family references. Their knitting is entwined with memories of his mother's gestures of protection, which included knitting for her children. *Sweaterman* is based on a cable sweater Mark's mother had made for him. His choice of acrylic yarn for the costumes echoes the yarn preferences of his mother and grandmother. *Patriot Man* evolved from a skein of red, white, and blue variegated acrylic yarn and the political conservatism of the town where he was living. *Y-Man* (named for the Y chromosome) is a businessman/superhero, after Mark's father.

Mark's career as a fiber artist began with weaving during the 1980s. His large-scale tapestries based on images from sports and pin-up magazines were also explorations of gender roles and heroism. Rendering action images through the time-consuming process of tapestry set up a contradiction in the viewer's mind in much the same way that Mark's knitted works do.

The mid 1990s found Mark sewing beads onto football trading cards, adding a "feminine" element to these masculine icons. He thought of these as "fetish

Bobble Man | Mark Newport | 2006 | hand-knit costume, worsted-weight yarn
Mark has created his own cast of "knitting superheroes." Their names and style of dress are inspired by pattern stitches.

Rawhide Kid | Mark Newport | 2004 | hand-knit costume, worsted-weight yarn
Mark reproduced the *Rawhide Kid*'s costume in great detail. Even the holsters and gloves are knit. This suit is part of his hand-knit series *Suits for Comic Book Characters*.

objects transformed by the hand-work process." Mark embroidered a series of superhero comic book covers after he asked himself, "If young men learned to embroider today, what images would they choose to work on?"

Mark's superhero quilts were based on the tradition of freedom quilts and made from reproductions of comic strips on paper with quilt binding and backing added. Embroidery or beading in selected frames transforms the heroes and calls the masculine stereotype into question.

In 2005, Mark was interested in performance art but not quite ready to plunge into it, so he had a series of still photos taken of himself poised for action in his knitted suits. "The photos are a way to take on the roles without an audience and to suggest what the hero might do in certain settings," he explained. Still questioning, he asked, "What do my heroes do? How do they operate every day? How do they fight or use their

powers?" A subsequent group of inkjet prints shows Mark in various relationships to the costumes.

In 2006, Mark performed in the *Batman, Rawhide Kid, Y-Man,* and *Sweaterman* suits at an art opening, interacting with visitors while superhero-type sounds emitted from an audio setup in his chest. He is currently doing some video work, animating the tableaux that appear in his photos and prints. He is also creating his own comic book, *The Adventures of Sweaterman*, in order to relate the origination myth of his new characters. Mark also plans on making more public appearances in his superhero suits. So be on the lookout for *Sweaterman*—his protective force field is available whenever you need it.

Knitting a Force Field 2 | Mark Newport | 2005 | digital print

Mark portrays himself as *Sweaterman*, one of his knitting superheroes. According to Mark, these heroes protect their charges by generating an invisible force field with their knitting. He is presently writing and illustrating *The Adventures of Sweaterman*, a comic book about this cast of knitting characters.

SSSK | Mark Newport | 2005 | digital print

In this print, Mark portrays himself as Spiderman knitting his costume onto his body, although he has not yet actually knit a Spiderman suit.

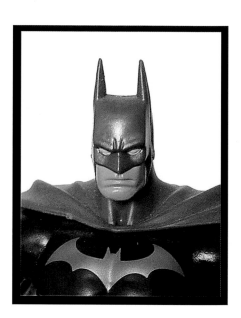

Batmen | Mark Newport | 2005 | digital print
Mark in his *Batman 2* costume joins a lineup of Batman action figures.

SSKOW | Mark Newport | 2005 | digital print
Mark's print shows him dressed as one of his knitting superheroes "talking shop" with Batman.

Janet Morton

Janet Morton, shown at work during her thirty-day installation *Newsflash: Madame Defarge Eat Your Heart Out*, a knitting ritual/performance that took place in a Toronto storefront in 1995. This installation included images of knitters, more than 1,000 balls of wool set into a false floor, vinyl text, and a television playing her "Rocknit Video." Each day, Janet would knit the newspaper headlines and other information into her *Newsflash Blanket*.

Viewers relate readily to Janet Morton's knitted works, which playfully examine everyday objects and events. This mixed-media sculptor and knitter delights in surprising her viewers by showing knitting in unlikely contexts. "My inspiration often comes from questions that I know don't have answers, or that intrigue me, fascinate, or disturb me," Janet says. "I try to figure some of it out by making art." How does time relate to value? How do we spend our time? How is value assigned to an object? What is beauty? Can work equal worth? Can I redeem the discarded? What do I value? Where does truth lie? These are some of the questions Janet ponders. Underlying her humorous works are thought-provoking critiques of excess and displaced sentimentality, which are aptly expressed through knitting and our time-honored traditions of making things for people we love.

Janet first learned to knit while she was an exchange student in Denmark. Her Danish classmates were astounded that she had never owned a pair of hand-knit socks. In short order, she was gifted with socks and knitting lessons, and immediately became an avid knitter. Later, as a fine arts student at York University, Toronto, she turned to knitting to create large-scale sculptures because her studio space was so small. She carved a pair of giant knitting needles and set to work with her hands and her irrepressible curiosity, discovering one of knitting's political aspects in the process. "I thought that the world could be changed if everyone started knitting their own socks," she recalled. "Then, they would repair their socks—they wouldn't go to the dollar store to buy another pair. When you invest, you care."

There has been a recent resurgence of interest in Janet's early work as knitting becomes more accepted as an art medium. In the early 1990s, Janet brought knitting into public view by placing large knitted works on outdoor monuments and public buildings. She had long admired the popular jumbo folk-art icons along the Trans-Canada Highway. "Most people feel alienated from a commemorative statue, and yet they eagerly embrace a giant snowman or a giant moose, or a giant lobster trap,"

Sweaterbike | Janet Morton | 1993 | hand-knit wool
The *Sweaterbike* is one of Janet's early sweaters created for inanimate objects.

Cardigan for a Giraffe | Janet Morton | 1993 | hand-knit wool
This unlikely garment is part of Janet's *Animal Apparel* series, which was displayed at the Toronto Zoo's Zooarts Festival in 2004. Janet intends the garments as a critique of our human tendency to assert personal aesthetics onto nature.

Work Socks for Patsy the Elephant | Janet Morton | 1999 | hand-knit wool
Janet's humorous *Animal Apparel* series was displayed at the Toronto Zoo's Zooarts Festival in 2004.

she said, in describing her frustrations while studying public sculpture. She created her own iconic image of quintessential Canadiana: a sixteen-foot-long, grey wool work sock. Draping it on public sculptures set up a visual equation between the bronze works and her knitting. The giant sock was followed by a giant- and normal-sized mitten pair hung on public buildings.

Next came a series of sweaters for inanimate objects, such as trees and bicycles, and her *Animal Apparel* series for inmates of the Toronto Zoo. This group of works includes *Cardigan for a Giraffe*, *Balaclava for a Rhino* (pink with a purple nose tassel), and *Work Socks for Patsy the Elephant*. "They are intended as critique," she says, "from my thoughts about the way we assert personal aesthetics onto nature (fashions for pet dogs, etc.) and from my

discomfort with the fact that exotic tropical animals are forced into artificial environments in Nordic climates." The group of works was exhibited at the 2004 Zooarts Festival at the Toronto Zoo.

During Janet's early forays into public art, people always asked about how much time she had spent knitting. Realizing the importance of questioning how we spend our time and energy, she concluded that knitting is a visual representation of a concrete measurement of time, and thus is an excellent artistic metaphor. "The kind of investment we make in knitting doesn't fit into the ways in which value and meanings are assigned to objects in our society," she says about one of the main themes in her artwork.

This line of thought resulted in an installation in which Janet used the low-tech medium of knitting to "slow down information," calling attention to the speeding-up of media and examining how time and handcraft production are valued. In an extremely ambitious undertaking, Janet installed herself in a storefront on one of Toronto's busiest streets where, for one month in 1995, six days a week from 10 AM to 5 PM, she performed ritual knitting of the headlines from the daily newspapers. Her setting included framed historical images of knitting on the walls and several thousand balls of wool set into a false floor. The continuously running "Rocknit Video" showed Janet and friends knitting in bizarre circumstances. Titled *Newsflash: Madame Defarge Eat Your Heart Out*, the installation evoked the memory of the

Newsflash Blanket, detail | Janet Morton | 1995 | hand-knit wool | 9' w x 23'

This blanket is the result of Janet's thirty-day knitting performance aimed at slowing down the media in the face of ever-accelerating technology.

legendary figure who recorded in her knitting names of those condemned to the guillotine, just as Janet similarly recorded current history. *Newsflash Blanket* contains a slice of history, from the bombings in Oklahoma City to a major-league baseball strike. She included personal items as time permitted: the weather, birthdays, her mood. "It was a grueling and amazing experience, and very much the personal political," Janet recalls. "I would guess that at least a thousand people a day would pass me. More on Saturdays." Many of her daily visitors showed her their knitting, or left her gifts of wool, poems, and homemade cookies.

In 1999, Janet began knitting small architectural studies, consisting of miniature woolen buildings sitting atop a ball of yarn. One of these morphed into one of her largest works. *Cozy*, a fitted covering for an empty cottage on Ward's Island, Toronto, originated from thoughts about home and homelessness. It was installed for one month to mark the 1999/2000 millennium. Janet pieced together 800 recycled white sweaters for the house cover, handknitting border trims around the window and door openings. More than 25,000 people traveled by ferry to visit the site. The work was reinstalled in 2000 over scaffolding in a Toronto park that is often frequented by homeless people.

Janet created *Cozy*'s imagined interior, *Untitled (Domestic Interior)*, in 2000 for an exhibition at The Textile Museum of Canada. She again used recycled sweaters with hand-knit details to cover household objects. Among its furniture and accessories, the room boasts a TV, a vacuum cleaner, a telephone, plants, and paintings. She even included a fuzzy teacup as a nod to Surrealist artist Meret Oppenheim's famous fur-lined teacup. The installation traveled to London and toured in Europe for five years.

Janet's more recent knitted installations deal with themes of recycling and include *Tending,* for which she knit a twelve-foot-tall anatomical heart surrounded by knitted vines and *Persistent Melody,* featuring objects knitted from her audio cassette tape collection. *Woollen Tree* is a knitted stage setting for a dance performance in which the choreographer and dancers, who were also knitters, worked on the piece onstage. A gallery of Janet's work can be seen on the Canadian artists' website www.ccca.ca.

Now the mother of a two-year-old son and an infant daughter, Janet relishes her parenting role. "It's an honor to watch someone discover the world and share in his excitement," she says. She has returned to knitting giant iconic images, as they are easily worked on in odd snatches of time. Initially, she set out to work at home in order not to miss any part of her son's early childhood, but she recently began renting studio space again, partly to protect her work from a very curious and busy boy. Since adapting to time and space constraints propels Janet in different directions with her work, it will be fascinating to see what comes next from her needles.

Above:

Cozy, front view | Janet Morton | 1999 | recycled wool sweaters, hand-knit trim, 250 plastic buttons, Velcro, and cotton lining
This warm, fitted covering was installed on a house on Ward's Island, Toronto, to mark the 1999/2000 millennium. Inspired by thoughts of home and homelessness, Janet constructed *Cozy* from more than 800 recycled sweaters; she handknit the window and door trims. The piece was re-installed over a scaffold in a Toronto park in the spring of 2000 for an event sponsored by The Textile Museum of Canada. In 2005, it was shown at Museum London.

Right:

Capitol | Janet Morton | 2004 | hand-knit wool | 9" tall
This small sculpture is part of Janet's series of architectural studies portraying well-known public buildings.

Tending | Janet Morton | 2003 | hand-knit heart, vines, and leaves, 2,500 recycled soda bottles | 12' tall
For her gallery installation on consumer excess and recycling, Janet knit a twelve-foot-tall, anatomically correct heart and trailing vines and leaves scaling a wall that she constructed from 2,500 plastic bottles.

John Krynick

Artistic breakthroughs come in unexpected ways. Fiber artist John Krynick is also an antiques dealer specializing in American Folk Art. In 1993, while perusing an auction-house catalog, his attention was riveted by a photo of a knitted wool letter that had been sent to President Andrew Johnson in 1868* by an inmate of the Washington Insane Asylum. Intrigued by the care that went into the knitting in contrast to the ranting message, and inspired by the potential power of the knitted word, John began knitting his own letters and mailing them to friends. "I sort of knew how to knit all along," he recalls. He taught himself more knitting skills in order to do the letters.

Knitting's portability was an advantage for him at the time, since he was a weaver without studio space to set up his loom. His first letters were small pieces in offbeat color combinations made with fine cotton yarns. They contain eccentric word breaks and his invented punctuation system of vertical and dotted lines. The texts came from his interests: he is a foodie and an excellent chef, and quotes liberally from his collection of nineteenth-century memorabilia: recipes, culinary history, and natural history. Often the messages are chosen for their visual puns on gay-related words, such as *Pansy*, which quotes a nineteenth-century naturalist; or the *Queen Cakes* sampler, which quotes an 1861 recipe.

The letters appealed to John's views that textiles are a form of language and that ordinary textiles should be considered art objects. Somewhat of a maverick about exhibiting his work, he prefers venues where people can handle the pieces. While he was knitting his intricate letters and samplers, he was also knitting twelve-inch squares, planting seeds on them, and leaving them outdoors to sprout and be discovered by chance.

Self | John Krynick | 2006 | machine-knit alpaca and wool | 5" x 7"
Self is John Krynick's machine-knit self-portrait.

Josh/Mexican | John Krynick | 2006–2007 | machine-knit acrylic, double-faced Jacquard technique | 10" x 12"
John stitched with the sewing machine to highlight images and details in both sections of this knitted diptych. *Photograph by Andy Wainwright*

Sunset Boulevard |
John Krynick | hand-knit
cotton and nylon thread |
16.5" x 16.5"
In this hand-knit "letter,"
John quotes the entire "Mr.
DeMille" speech of Norma
Desmond from the film
Sunset Boulevard.

The fact that John was a male practicing a domestic art form lent additional meaning to his laboriously hand-knit samplers with their subtle messages of identity and politics. "My interest is in a type of textile production that's associated with domesticity—with a traditional feminine role. But as a gay man, I questioned those types of stereotypical gender-assigned roles," he explains.

In recent works on the knitting machine, the domestic connection has shifted somewhat as he produces works with imagery and a broader social commentary. He enjoys the nineteenth-century notions of the machine and the home industrial process. "The domestic relationship changed when the knitting machine came into the picture: man as controller of machine, woman of the hearth and home—I like playing with those assumptions and mixing them up."

Adjusting to the machine brought unexpected frustrations as he learned its capabilities and limitations. Originally, he thought it would be effective for his letters but didn't like the result. He developed a new body of work based on repeating manipulated images from photos and the media, and did lots of sampling to find yarns that would work to his satisfaction. He settled on using fine threads that he can blend to create his unusual color mixes.

One group of works features images of beauty queens photographed from the TV screen at the moment their names were called. Grids containing repetitions of faces—his own and his friends—or images from his collection of nineteenth-century circus performer photos dominate other works. He utilizes Cat Mazza's KnitPro service to digitize his manipulated images, then programs them into his Brother KH970 computer and knits a double-faced Jacquard fabric.

In addition to manipulating imagery, John manipulates his knitted fabrics. He pieces, stitches, stuffs, and distorts them into curious objects. He pins them to his studio wall, enjoying an informal presentation that allows people to touch them. He also posts them on his weblog to get feedback from readers. Edges are left unfinished to emphasize the ephemeral nature of textiles, "incorporating into the piece its own disintegration, or possibility for change." He recently began embroidering on some of the pieces. "Well I'm calling it embroidery, it's my take on embroidery and related to embroidery—just like my knitting is related to knitting. In my mind, I think of it all as painting and drawing."

In honor of turning fifty in 2007, John cut his hair and shaved off his trademark handlebar moustache, shedding a hippie-artist persona for the disguise of a middle-aged businessman. Until recently, his studio was located in the Hudson, New York, antiques shop that housed the business he owns with his partner, Francis. In the winter of 2007, they closed the shop and compressed inventory and studio into their already-crowded Woodstock home, in preparation for a move to Philadelphia later in the year.

A native of New Jersey, John received his BFA degree at Philadelphia College of Art and his MFA from Cranbrook Academy of Art in 1984. "At that point, fiber art was deeply entrenched in its craft roots," he says. "In the current climate of contemporary art, references to cloth or textile are much more prevalent. Textiles are such a part of our lives, it seems normal to me that they are part of the contemporary dialogue in art."

John draws on ancient textiles, domestic textile history, art history, and nineteenth-century science and philosophy for some of his inspiration. Objects in his own collection and the objects he encounters in business inspire him as well. "Folk art and Americana—I look at it all the time. I'm making textiles that talk about textiles and what textiles do and how they are everywhere. This textile reference allows anyone to have access into the work because everyone has some association with textiles."

Handwork projects-in-process in his studio include knitted rugs based on a nineteenth-century ravel-knit technique used by the Shakers. John's versions consist of his machine-knit rejects cut into strips and stitched down on ticking. Experimental works with unusual materials include crocheted spiral forms in ribbon and some large-scale knitted works in newspaper. *The New York Times* series compresses one day, one week, and one month of the news into intriguing knitted artifacts. John creates a ball of "yarn" with rolled newspaper wrapped with thread and knits it on handmade dowel-rod needles. He is working on a group of giant-sized newspaper garments based on antique doll clothes patterns. Each garment is about seven feet tall and is free-standing.

Since 2005, John has been documenting his work and life and revealing his creative process in a weblog project, http://napkinplease.blogspot.com/. Subtitled "An artist with a knitting machine makes stuff, makes stuff up, makes dinner, makes a mess," it covers the range of his interests in food, art, popular culture, travel, and of course, knitting.

*The 1868 letter is published in the catalogue *Talkative Textiles* for the 1992 exhibition curated by Mary Hunt Kahlenberg.

Ravel-knit Rug | John Krynick | 2005 | machine-knit, unraveled, stitched wool, cotton ticking | 60" x 46"
John puts his machine-knit samples and "rejects" to good use in rugs made with a technique invented by the Shakers. He cuts machine-knit fabric into strips and stitches the strips onto a heavy cotton backing. *Photograph by Andy Wainwright*

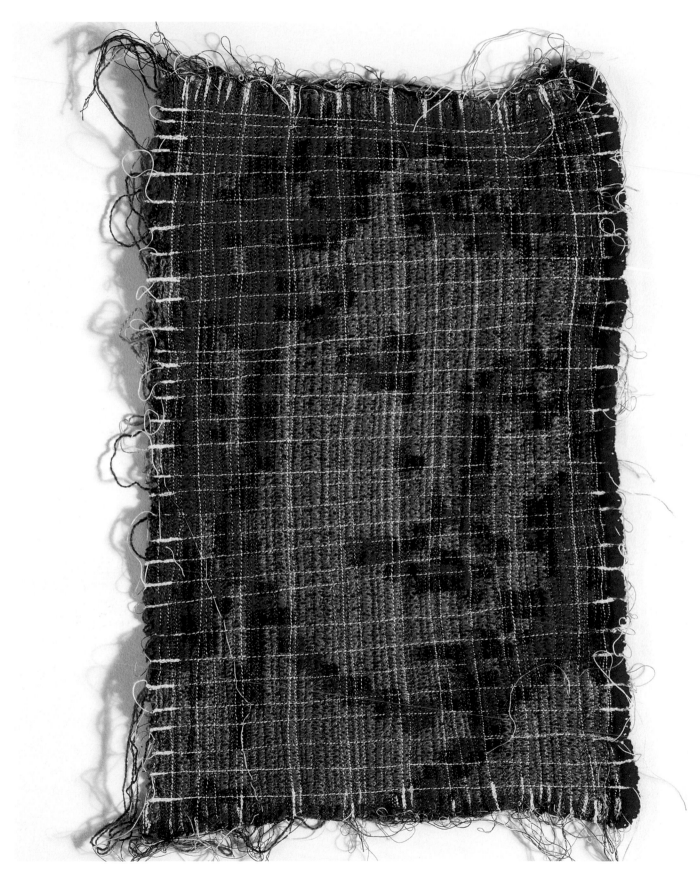

Fran | John Krynick | 2006–2007 | machine-knit acrylic and cotton | 10" x 15"
John added stitching to transform the surface of this machine-knitted piece that started out as a digital photo of his partner.
Photograph by Andy Wainwright

Circassian | John Krynick | machine-knit cotton, dimensions variable
John can arrange these small face images into various configurations. He often utilizes digitized photographs in his machine-knit works.

One Week |
John Krynick |
2007 | hand-knit
newspaper wrapped
with string |
48" x 32" x 2.5"
John has composed an
entire week's issues
of *The New York Times*
into an impressive
knitted artifact.

Barb Hunt

Barb Hunt. *Photograph by Jerry Browne*

Barb Hunt's knitted works offer gestures of healing. Her ongoing project since 1998 has been to knit precise replicas of anti-personnel devices, or land mines, in soft shades of pink wool. From a distance, they appear to be curious, benign objects, but up close, they deliver an emotional impact. By replacing objects of destruction with her own handwork, she refocuses our attention on the value of "small personal gestures that can accumulate into a declaration of caring and hope." She explains, "Knitting is a way to cope with grief and horror, and it helps me to cope on a personal and political level. It is art as healing, protection, and care, all of which are inherent in wool and knitting."

Barb began knitting the replicas in 1998 when a Canada Council grant took her to Paris for knitting research. While there, she visited The Pyramid of Shoes, an annual protest against land mines. "The Pyramid of Shoes is a big event where Parisians bring pairs of shoes (tied together so they can be given to charity later) in solidarity with those who have lost limbs due to land mines. There were people who explained how the mines worked and the devastation they caused, a display of handmade prosthetics, and some crafts made by victims of mines." Barb then researched land mines and issues of war at the War Museum in Paris, and located various sources for obtaining detailed specifications for these devices. "Sometimes people in the art world assume that I am against the military," Barb says, "but I'm not—I'm against war and these terrible weapons."

Not all of the mines' crenellated metallic surfaces are easy to reproduce. Barb makes use of knit and purl stitches to create raised surfaces and surfaces that recede. Her replicas are as accurate as possible, including tiny knitted fuses and nuts and bolts. Images of the real thing often accompany her exhibitions. So far, she has replicated seventy out of more than 350 available devices.

Ladder at Trout River, NF | Barb Hunt | 1996–1998 | hand-knit yarn | 18" x 20'
Barb's knitted ladder placed along a riverbank expresses "the imaginary pleasure of rising above the earthly plane and working in tiny increments to bring myself to a new place." *Photograph by Jerry Browne*

antipersonnel, detail of installation | Barb Hunt | hand-knit yarn
This section of Barb's knitted land mine installation includes: Argentina pressure-activated mine (left), Netherlands bounding fragmentation mine (top), Vietnam pressure-activated mine (center front), and Pakistan pressure-activated mine (right). The details are accurate and even include tiny knitted nuts and bolts. *Photograph by Art Gallery of Ontario*

Stake Mines | Barb Hunt | 1998 to present (ongoing) | hand-knit yarn
Stake Mines is a portion of Barb's hand-knit installation, *antipersonnel*. The replicas of land mines are accurately scaled to life-sized dimensions. Barb began this work in 1998 and so far has knit more than seventy out of 350 different types of antipersonnel land mines. Various kinds of wool and yarn are the only materials that Barb uses; the stuffing consists of remnants of these pink yarns. *Photograph by Art Gallery of Ontario*

Knitting's slowness and attention to detail seems an appropriate counterpoint to the harsh reality of the mines. "It is in complete opposition to what these terrible things are made for," Barb says. "They are cheaply manufactured for instantaneous destruction. According to the International Campaign to Ban Landmines, there is a mine-explosion victim somewhere in the world every twenty minutes. I think, 'It's happening right now.' I'm brought into the present tense in a way that is emotional and difficult. I can't knit them every day."

The first section of Barb's *antipersonnel* installation was exhibited in 2001 in the Royal Military College of Canada Museum, where the docents were military students. "They have been among some of the strongest supporters of this work, because they are going to have to face the danger of mines when they are posted overseas," she says. The exhibit was part of the Museopathy Project in Kingston, Ontario, in which artists were invited to make interventions into the city's museums. It was initiated by the Agnes Etherington Arts Centre and curated by Jim Drobnick and Jennifer Fisher. This portion of *antipersonnel* was given a permanent home at the Agnes Etherington Arts Centre in Kingston, Ontario.

Barb was born in upstate New York and grew up in rural Ontario. Handwork was ever-present in her Irish family, as was a sense of community involvement. Barb's grandmothers both made quilts, and as a child in the 1950s, Barb participated in a 4-H club. She learned enough knitting technique from her mother to the knit the six-inch square required to earn a badge. Later, as a fine arts student in the 1970s, Barb knit her own clothing designs. She received her BFA degree in sculpture and printmaking from the University of Manitoba, since at that time craft media were not yet accepted as fine art. In the MFA program at Concordia University, Montreal, she studied fibers and became serious about incorporating knitting into her artwork.

On a 1999 research trip to Ireland, Barb studied the region's knitting history and the history of individual stitches, and met knitters in the Aran Islands. "I found reassurance that I was on the right track, and that knitting is art," she says. "The Aran stitches are inspired by nature and the environment. Women there were originally taught to knit as a means to earn money, but they invented stitches and patterns and developed an artform that is not appreciated, because it's used for clothing." Barb uses some Aran stitches in the mine replicas. For the Japanese mine, she used the moss stitch pattern, called "life-giving" in Gaelic.

Barb is an Associate Professor of Art at Memorial University of Newfoundland and lives in the small town of Corner Brook, which she finds inspiring for its rich tradition of domestic textile practices. "Knitting is in the air I breathe out here," she says. Her partner, Jerry Browne, is a Newfoundlander, descended from many generations of fishermen. His mother Geraldine knits, as do most women in the community. Barb never ceases to be impressed by this amazing woman who raised eleven children in a house without electricity for many years, baked seven loaves of bread every day in a wood stove, knitted all their socks, and sometimes even helped her husband by fishing with him! "There is an atmosphere of practicality and of care for the material world here," Barb says. "It is away from big cities, pollution, and worry about terrorism, but not away from war. A disproportionately high percentage of Newfoundlanders serve in the Canadian armed forces, particularly in Afghanistan."

Knitting as a healing gesture has been part of Barb's work for a long time. During a 1989 artist's residency in Banff, Alberta, Barb knit small surprise gifts for friends, leaving them anonymously. She called the improbable objects she made "aids for living." They were soft, stuffed replacements for items lost or needed, such as a black light aglow with purple beads for an artist who couldn't locate one for an exhibition, or a tongue for a friend who wished she could speak more eloquently. In an ongoing knitted work called *Solace*, Barb knits bandages in a gesture intended to heal wounds through knitting, and as a testament to the history of women who knit bandages in Europe and North America during times of war. Many of her knit works are on her website, www.barbhunt.com.

Barb credits feminism with giving artists permission to use practices from the domestic sphere in their artwork. "Knitting has long had a strong association with women's work, even though it was done by men during the Middle Ages. I am stating my gender through my art. I knit. This is pink wool. I'm a feminist and a woman and won't pretend otherwise."

Opposite page, top:

Pall | Barb Hunt | 1996–1998 | hand-knitted yarn | 7' x 3.5'
Another of Barb's ongoing knitted works consists of small squares knit in the style of old-time hand-knit bandages. The installation can be arranged into many different configurations. Here, it is shown in a 1998 exhibition as a pall, or protective covering, for the deceased. *Photograph by Sheila Spence*

Opposite page, bottom:

Pall, detail | Barb Hunt | 1996–1998 | hand-knitted yarn

Solace | Barb Hunt |
2007 | hand-knit yarn |
1' x 30'
In this version of
Barb's knitted bandage
installation, the knit
squares are configured
as a long strip that
wraps around the gallery.
Photograph by Tom Hurley

Amnesty | Barb Hunt | 1993 | hand-knit yarn | 6" x 48"
Barb replicates the style of knitted bandages from the mid-nineteenth century to form this rifle-shaped work. *Photograph by Paul Litherland*

Karen Searle

by Kari Cornell

Karen Searle and her knit wire sculpture *Woman Within II*. Photograph by Doroth Mayer

Karen Searle's studio in St. Paul, Minnesota, is filled with sculptures crafted from wire, bamboo, wood, handmade paper, shredded money, even horsehair. Wire chair and garment forms appear suspended in mid air. Works in mixed media with found objects, the found objects themselves, and spools of thread cover every available surface. And then there's the artist at work: Karen's knitting needles seem to move along with the cadence of her speech as she talks about her art.

Each stitch, whether it was knit or crocheted, exists as its own entity in Karen's intriguing sculptures. These defined stitches, carefully chosen, are an integral part of the whole. To Karen, technique is more than just the means to an end; technique is an important part of the particular work's concept and meaning. "I strive for a marriage of technique and material in service to a concept. The technical aspects should support the metaphoric content of the work. When we put something of ourselves into a piece, that energy is conveyed to the viewers, who are free to add their own interpretations to it," says Karen.

Karen considers herself a sculptor. When she takes the time to knit or crochet her vessels, thrones, and figures, she imbues each work with "an invisible layer of meaning" that comes from the process itself. "The act of knitting connects me symbolically with all women who have ever knitted, and the investment of time in constructing the piece in that careful way sets it apart from this society's emphasis on technology and mass production," she explains.

Karen began to knit and crochet in college. She had rebelled against the notion of following patterns to the letter from the start, and after taking a workshop from the late Elizabeth Zimmermann around 1974, Karen started designing her own patterns. Learning to knit and crochet led Karen to weaving, which intrigued her. After moving to Minnesota in 1969 and taking classes offered through the Minnesota Weaver's Guild, she became immersed in weaving, doing commission

Body Bag X: Patched-In | Karen Searle | 2005 | freeform knitting with telephone wire | 14" tall
Karen's ongoing *Body Bag* series of torso/containers portrays aspects of women's lives. This torso was worked in a freeform knitting technique. *Photograph by Peter Lee*

Woman Within II |
Karen Searle |
2006 | hand-knit
wire | 28" tall
Karen utilizes the
transparent qualities
of knitted wire in her
forms within forms.

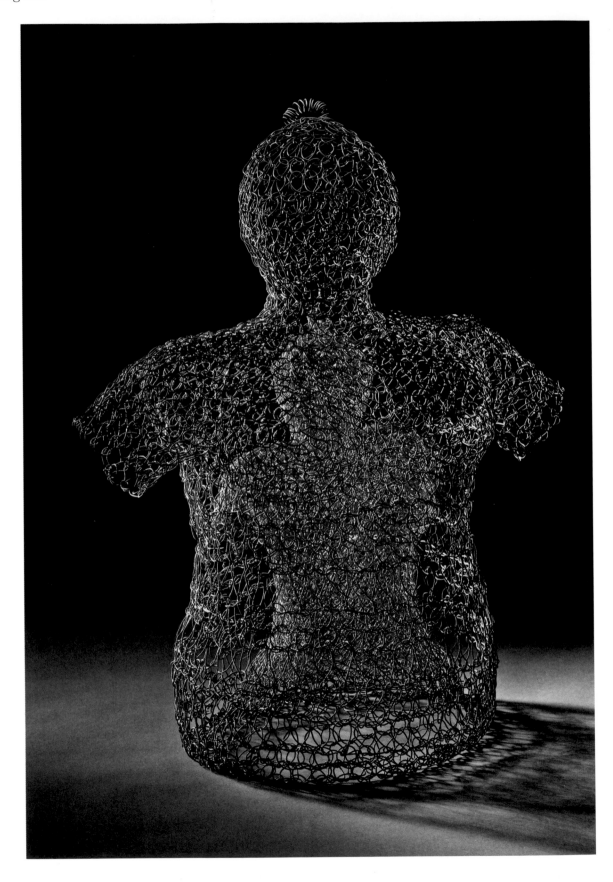

work, teaching, writing, and publishing on the subject—all while raising two kids! As her weaving moved toward complex, three-dimensional forms, however, Karen realized that the figurative works she envisioned would be easier to achieve using knitting or crochet, two techniques that offer endless possibilities for subtle shaping. Attending a Mary Walker Phillips workshop on creative knitting in the 1980s propelled Karen further along the art-knitting path. She retired from her publishing career in 1996, and enrolled in graduate school, earning her MFA degree from the Minneapolis College of Art and Design in 1999.

Today, she explores many different aspects of knitting and crochet, both separately and in combination, in order to assert the validity of women's work and the feminine view. Karen's ironic sense of humor permeates her *Body Bag* series of bags and vessels knit in the shape of the female form. The *Body Bags* and her middle-aged female figures represent Karen's feelings about being an aging woman in a society that's fixated on youth, and making the decision to accept and embrace the changes age brings to her body. "I often create figures based on the Jungian idea of the body as a container for aspects of the self, and the container-as-body seemed a fitting vehicle for this ongoing series about women surviving whatever life throws at them."

Her *Goddess Throne* series is an extension of the body metaphor. "An empty chair suggests the absence of a body." Her empty wire garments are extensions of same idea—together with their shadows, they show traces of the energy of the absent wearer. "The *Thrones* evoke the presence of the feminine spirit from ancient times," Karen says. The folk-art-inspired *Homage to the Goddess: Creation*, worked around a chair frame, integrates knitting, crochet, and tablet weaving with mythological symbolism. The ethereal wire-knit *Spirit Throne* honors the feminine spirit. The natural linen *Crone's Throne* (in process) honors women over fifty.

In Karen's work, the materials she decides to use are just as important as the technique and the process. "I learn what a material will and will not do, and ideas of what it can express come as I experiment. 'The

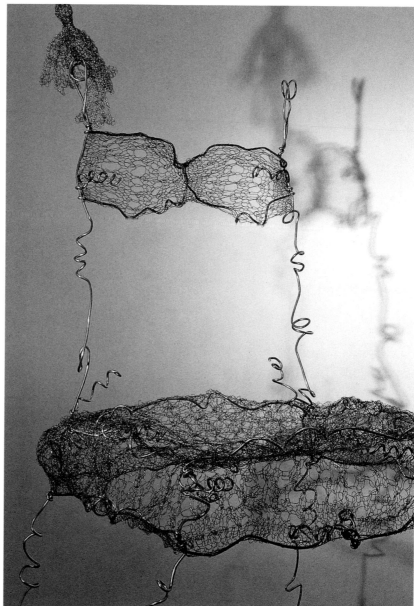

Spirit Throne | Karen Searle | 1999 | hand-knit copper wire and bent aluminum wire | 4' tall

In celebration of the female spirit, Karen created an ethereal wire "throne" adorned with a copper bird about to take flight.

material talks to me' sounds a bit strange, but that is what happens. The fiber moving through my hands evokes images of the forms it can take." A material's history may also lend additional meaning to a work for Karen. She often chooses to render a female form in linen, knowing that women have always played a role in the growing and processing of its fiber. She associates her use of wire with contemporary, technological society. She generally doesn't sit down and plan a piece in detail. Starting one of her meticulously shaped female figures at the ankle, she

Prime of Life | Karen Searle | 1998 | hand-knit linen | 8" tall
Karen's humorous portraits of middle-aged women are a hallmark of her
sculptural works in knitting and crochet. *Photograph by Dana Wheelock*

and their textile traditions for most of her life. In 1980, she spent time in Guatemala studying the country's brocaded weavings and co-authored a book on the subject. She has led textile tours of the country since 1993. After several trips to Korea, she was inspired to lead a textile tour there as well. "My love of folk art influences my work sometimes directly, as in the use of color and imagery, but more often indirectly, through the desire to make something well regardless of the time it takes."

In addition to creating and exhibiting art and writing about artists and art knitting, Karen teaches classes and workshops and serves as a mentor to emerging artists through the Women's Art Registry of Minnesota. Her website, www.karensearle.com, displays a gallery of her work. Karen also takes great pleasure in curating exhibits as an integral part of maintaining a balanced and fulfilling life as an artist. "Curating offers a different set of challenges and involves research, writing, and a chance to broaden my knowledge of the field."

Back in Karen's studio, she's hard at work on a series of life-sized wire forms that combine the interplay of their line-drawing effects with the shadows they cast. Image and shadow are also an important element

works upward, and the shape and length of the leg will determine the proportions for the rest of the body.

Karen draws inspiration from her textile-related travels. As someone who was originally trained as a translator, she has been interested in other cultures

in a group of knitted, crocheted, and lace works on the theme of aging and memory. She represents the fiber arts in a group of women artists in their sixties and seventies who explore aging in different art media and exhibit together. "Art is finding the essence, or the metaphor in a personal emotion or experience, and putting it forth in a form that both summarizes and communicates it," Karen says. "That's not always an easy job. We accomplish it through following our process."

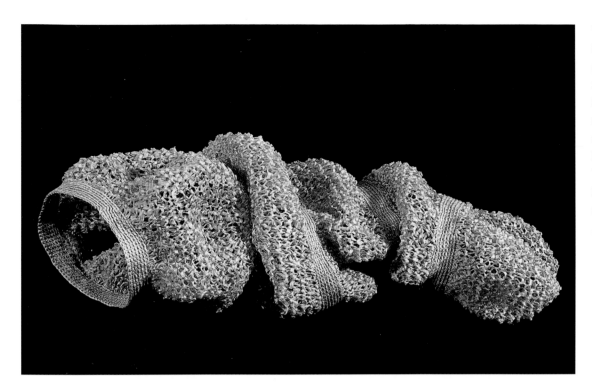

Vessel | Karen Searle | 2006 | hand-knit flax paper, crocheted linen rug warp | 36" long
Karen contrasted the open, airy paper knit with dense areas of crocheted linen in this vessel form. The tight crocheted bands help maintain the vessel's shape. *Photograph by Petronella Ytsma*

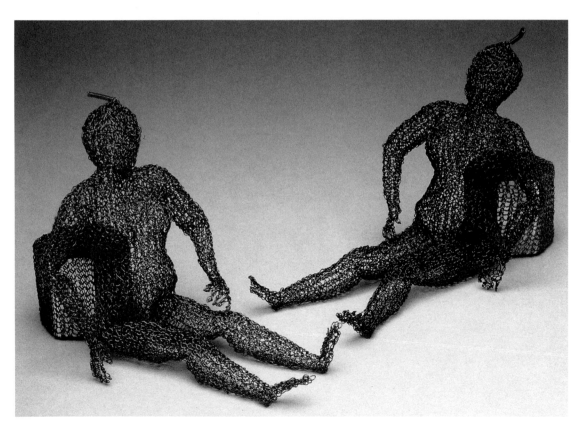

Mini Wire Women | Karen Searle | 2006 | hand-knit copper wire | 7" tall
Karen's diminutive wire figures are knit on size 000 lace needles. The figures are meticulously shaped and have lifelike movement. *Photograph by Peter Lee*

Bark Quilt III | Karen Searle | 2005 | birch bark, glass beads, hand-knit silk | 13" x 28"

Karen's ongoing series of *Bark Quilts* are meditative works celebrating the beauty of nature. She makes the quilts by mending, beading, and piecing together bits of found birch bark. She thinks of them as metaphors for women's work and women's lives: "as women we salvage, piece together, mend, and adorn our objects and our relationships." *Photograph by Petronella Ytsma*

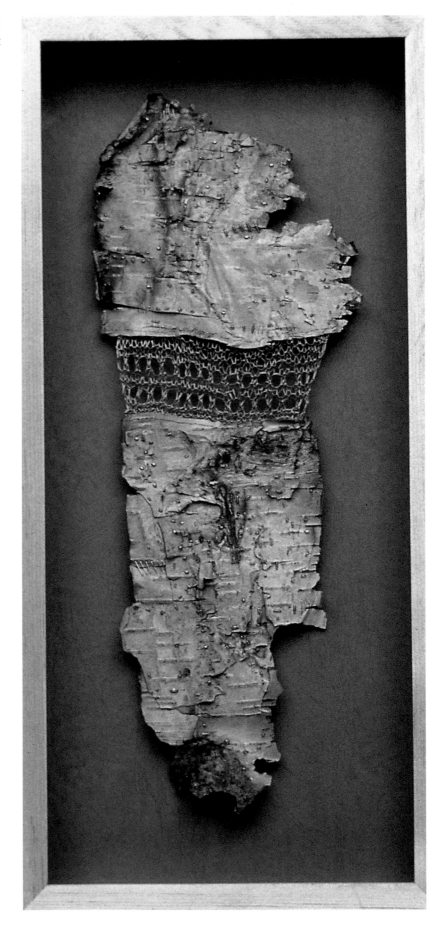

Essence Part 5: Formal Dress | Karen Searle | 2006 | finger knit and crochet steel wire, shadow | life-sized garment and accessories Karen's *Essence* installation of knit and crocheted wire garments and their shadows depicts events in the life of a mythical woman. The heavy wire worked at this scale resembles a line drawing in space interacting with its shadow. *Photograph by Petronella Ytsma*

Glossary of Specialized Knitting Techniques and Other Terms

Collapse-weave fabrics
Fabrics made in weave structures that emphasize the flexibility and movement of yarns. Using yarns made with opposing twists (see left- and right-twist) directly affects the amount of "collapse."

Diagonal knitting
Katharine Cobey defines diagonal knitting as "a way of working and shaping where the knitted rows are constructed at a forty-five-degree angle to the horizontal and vertical edges of the piece." A diagonal piece can be worked as a bias strip by increasing at one side and decreasing at the other side, or as a diamond shape by starting at a point and forming the shape through increasing and then decreasing, either in the center or at the edges.

Double knitting
A method of constructing a stockinette-stitch tube while knitting back and forth on straight needles. An even number of stitches is required. Each row is worked in the same manner: knit one stitch, slip the next stitch as if to purl; repeat across. The resulting piece will have stockinette stitch on both sides, and when the needles are removed, it will also have two separate layers.

Entrelac
Kathryn Alexander explains entrelac as "a diagonal knitting technique that involves small units of squares knit on opposing bias. One row slants to the left, the next row slants to the right."

Felt
A fabric of compressed fibers, usually wool, that is formed through the use of heat, moisture, and agitation.

Felted knitting
A knitted wool fabric that has undergone the felting process to shrink and mat the wool fibers.

Fulling
A finishing process for wool fabrics using soap, hot water, and agitation that results in controlled shrinkage; the final stage of felting.

Freeform knitting
Debbie New defines freeform knitting as "a technique for building up a knitted fabric piece in various directions, yarns, and stitches." It is a modular approach to knitting, working in small, improvised units that are assembled later. Some artists include crochet in their freeform pieces to add additional texture.

I-cord
A cord knitted on two double-pointed needles. To make the cord, cast on three stitches and knit them. For subsequent rows, do not turn the work, merely slide the stitches to the right and knit them again. After a few rows, the stitches will form a tube.

Knitting-on (yarn painting)
Knitting-on is a means of attaching a decorative piece of knitting-in-progress at intervals to the edge or surface of an existing knitted piece. The decorative addition may be a flat strip or an I-cord, and the process can be done by hand or on the knitting machine. At the point of attachment, stitches are picked up in the already-knit piece and worked together with the stitches of the decorative addition.

Left- and right-twist (S- and Z-twist) yarns
These terms designate the direction in which a yarn has been spun. Left, or S-twist, indicates that the thread was spun counterclockwise; right, or Z-twist, indicates clockwise spinning. The direction of twist in a yarn can affect the texture of a knitted or woven fabric.

Resist-patterning
Designs formed during the process of dyeing or painting fabrics by applying a substance or physical treatment that prevents the dyes or paints from penetrating the fabric in selected areas.

Shibori

The Japanese term for the resist patterning created in dyed fabrics by binding, stitching, twisting, or knotting areas of the fabric before dyeing.

Short-row shaping

A means of creating a bump or bulge in a knitted fabric, such as in the heel of a sock. To form a pair of short rows, knit partway across the fabric, turn the work, and knit partway back. Turn the work again, and finish the row as usual.

Lisa/Zoso Sweater and **Straight Edge/Poseur Skirt** | Lisa Anne Auerbach | 2005 | machine knit wool The sweater logo is based on a sweater worn by Jimmy Page of Led Zeppelin. Lisa reworked the "ZOSO" logo to resemble her name. The skirt says "anti-stupidity, pro-positive, pro-alertness, anti-stupidity, poseur," words from a song by Minor Threat that outlines ideas about "straight edge." Lisa says, "I thought that such a prescriptive approach to lifestyle wasn't very punk rock. And in punk rock, about the worst thing one can be is a poseur . . . so I knit the word into the skirt."

How Mother Dressed Me | Karen Searle | 2008 | hand-knit copper wire | installation of 8" high child's dresses
Karen juxtaposes her miniature knit dresses with images of her own childhood wardrobe in this work about aging and memory.

About the Author

Karen Searle is an artist and a writer whose knitted and crocheted sculptures have been exhibited widely over the past twenty-five years. She has presented workshops and lectures on knitting and weaving in the United States and abroad. Karen has co-authored two books on weaving and published books on cultural traditions in weaving, knitting, and crochet under the Dos Tejedoras imprint from 1976 through 1995. She has written extensively about artists and the arts for publications in the United States, Europe, and Korea.